بين الطراز
Between Forms

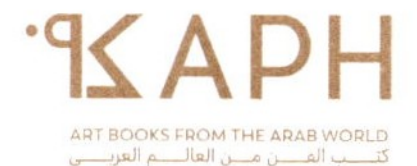

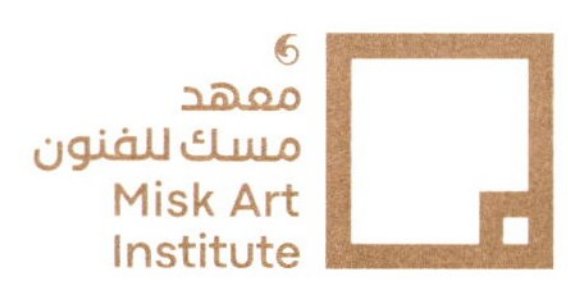

سلسـلة المعـارض الفرديـة
Solo Series

بسمه الشثري، مدير عام إدارة التقييم الفني وكبير القيمين الفنيين
Basma Alshathry, Director of Curatorial Department and Chief Curator

As we embark on the second iteration of Misk Art Institute's Solo Series, we honor the remarkable contributions of two pioneering Saudi artists: Khaleel Hassan Khaleel and Mohammed Alresayes. In this thriving cultural era within the Kingdom of Saudi Arabia, it remains imperative that we document and pay tribute to the influential figures who have significantly shaped our art scene.

The Solo Series continues its mandate to highlight pioneering Saudi artists via a platform for in-depth exploration of their unique creative practices. Khaleel Hassan Khaleel, a painter from Jizan on the Red Sea coast, has developed a distinct approach to his work, which he terms "Dreamism." This approach draws upon his personal and local heritage as a powerful driving force. The thirty-seven works in his solo exhibition, *The Whisper of Dreams*, invite viewers into a dreamlike realm where the boundaries of reality blur, reflecting both the complexities of Khaleel's inner and outer worlds and the rich cultural heritage of his homeland.

Similarly, Mohammed Alresayes's work is deeply rooted in his local Nadji heritage, and he has dedicated his artistic practice to reinterpreting the architectural elements of his hometown. His paintings serve as poignant reminders of the significance of local culture while also nurturing a sense of identity

في النسـخة الثانية من «سلسـلة المعـارض الفردية» التي ينظّمها معهد مسك للفنون، يسعدنا أن نحتفي بفنانين بارزين من أعلام الفن السعودي، خليل حسن خليـل ومحمد الرصيص. ففي ظـل الحيوية الثقافية التي تشـهدها المملكة العربية السـعودية اليوم، تبرز أهمية التركيز على الفنانين المؤثرين وتوثيق بصماتهم العميقة في رسـم معالم المشـهد الفني السـعودي وصياغة هويته البصرية المميزة.

تواصل «سلسـلة المعـارض الفرديـة» مهمتها في إبراز رّواد الفن السـعودي واستكشـاف عوالمهم الإبداعيـة الفريدة، وفـي هذا الإطـار، يقدّم معرض «قـد سـمعنا ما قُلـتَ فـي الأحـلامِ» للفنـان خليل حسن خليل سبعة وثلاثين عملاً من أعماله، تعكس تأثّره العميـق بواقعـه، كما تكشـف عـن فلسـفته الفنيـة الخاصة التي أطلـق عليها اسـم «الحُلمية»، والتي تسـتمد إلهامها من التراث الإنسـاني والعربي، بالإضافـة إلـى الإرث المحلـي لمسـقط رأس الفنان -منطقـة جـازان-. يدعو هـذا المعرض الـزوّار إلى الانغمـاس في عالمٍ حُلمـيّ تتلاشـى فيه الحدود بيـن الواقع والمخيّلة، وتتجلّى فيه الأبعاد النفسـية والوجدانيـة فـي تفاعل وثيق مـع التراث الإنسـاني والثقافة المحليـة الغنية.

وفـي إطار آخـر، يُقدّم معـرض «بيـن الطراز» عشـرين عمـلاً للفنـان الدكتـور محمـد الرصيص؛ تُظهر مكامن التجذر العميـق له في التراث النجدي، وقراءتـه المعاصرة للعناصـر المعمارية التي شـكّلت هوية مدينتـه، ويؤكد الرصيص مـن خـلال أعماله

and continuity with his homeland. Through the twenty works exhibited in his solo exhibition, *Between Forms*, we gain an appreciation for the intricate relationship between architecture and community, as Alresayes captures the essence of his surroundings in a contemporary context.

Both Khaleel and Alresayes, each with their own unique styles, exemplify how local culture profoundly influences creative expression. They embody the spirit of an artistic community that has been instrumental in building a distinct Saudi visual identity. Their works not only contribute to the narrative of the Saudi art scene, but also resonate with universal themes, inviting dialogue and reflection within a broader art historical context.

Misk Art Institute remains committed to preserving and promoting Saudi art history and highlighting its historic figures in order to ensure that future generations can explore and draw inspiration from the rich legacy of Saudi artists. The Solo Series serves as an essential archive that safeguards the vibrancy of the Kingdom's cultural landscape, as we continue to honor the past while looking forward to the future of Saudi artistic expression.

على ثراء الثقافة المحلية، ويخلق إحساساً بالهوية والانتماء، ويكشف عن العلاقة المترابطة بين العمارة والمجتمع، ساعياً إلى إعادة إحياء ملامح المكان ضمن سياق معاصر.

كلا الفنانين يقفان على ضفاف أسلوبهما الفريد والمختلف، ويقدّمان نموذجاً حيّاً يكشف عن جوانب تأثير الثقافة المحلية على التعبير الإبداعي، ويجسّدان روح الوسط الفني الذي لعب دوراً محورياً في تشكيل الهوية البصرية السعودية الأصيلة. كما أن أعمالهما لا تقتصر على إثراء السردية الفنية السعودية فحسب، بل تنصت لصدى الموضوعات العالمية، وتفتح فضاءات للحوار والتأمل في سياق تاريخ الفن العالمي الأوسع.

واحتفاءً بتاريخ الإبداع الفني في المملكة، واستشرافًا للآفاق الإبداعية الواعدة يكرّس معهد مسك للفنون التزامه في إبراز هذا التاريخ والحفاظ عليه وتسليط الضوء على روّاده وشخصياته التاريخية، بهدف تمكين الأجيال القادمة من استكشاف واستلهام هذا الإرث الغني، وتأتي «سلسلة المعارض الفردية» لتسهم بشكل فعّال في توثيق المشهد الثقافي السعودي، مُعزّزةً دورها كأرشيف نابض بالحياة يعكس تطور الفن والثقافة في المملكة؛ هي بمثابة جسر حي يربط بين إرث الماضي ورؤى المستقبل، مستعرضةً مسارات الإبداع التي تشكل هوية الثقافة السعودية المعاصرة.

بين الطراز
Between Forms

آرام العجاجي وندى العرادي
Aram Alajaji and Nada Alaradi

In the Saudi Arabian art scene, Mohammed Alresayes is a pioneering figure, renowned for the flattened visual character of his paintings. His works pay homage to the rich cultural tapestry and architectural heritage of Najd, the region where he was born and raised. The artist's distinctive angular style captures Saudi Arabian heritage through an innovative abstract lens that he developed early in his career. *Between Forms* features twenty of Alresayes's paintings and drawings that exemplify his approach to flatness through two interconnected themes: traditional architecture and cultural practices.

Architecture, particularly Najdi elements and traditional mud houses, play a central role in the artist's practice. His fascination with these structures began during his studies in a master's program in the United States in 1981, a time that coincided with the dramatic urban transformation of Riyadh. Beginning in the late 1960s, the city's masterplan led to the emergence of modern villas and concrete houses. While preserving many historical areas, the plan called for significant changes to the city's urban landscape and architectural heritage.[1] In the collective consciousness, this shift reclassified mud houses from "ordinary" to "traditional" homes, marking a significant societal shift.

يُعد محمد الرصيص أحـد أبرز الشـخصيات الرائدة في السـاحة الفنية السـعودية، وقد اشـتهر بالطابع البصـري -المسـطح- للوحاتـه، والتـي يحتفي فيها بالنسـيج الثقافـي الغني والتـراث المعمـاري المميز لمنطقة نجد حيث وُلد وترعرع. وقد صور الرصيص بأسـلوبه الحادّ مختلف عناصر التراث السعودي من خـلال عدسةٍ تجريدية مبتكـرة طورها منـذ بدايات مسيرته الفنية. ويضم معرض «بين الطراز» مجموعة مختارة مـن أعماله الفنية، تتكوّن مـن عشـرين لوحة ورسـمة تحضيريـة، تعكـس طابعه البصـري المتميز -المسطح- من خلال موضوعين مترابطين: العمارة التقليديـة التـي تجسّـد هوية المـكان والممارسـات الثقافيـة التي تعبّر عـن روح المجتمع.

شـكّلت العمـارة، وخاصة العناصـر النجديـة والبيـوت الطينيـة التقليدية، محـوراً أساسـياً فـي الممارسـة الفنيـة لمحمـد الرصيـص، الـذي تعمّـق فـي استكشـافها منـذ أيـام دراسـته للماجسـتير في الولايـات المتحـدة الأمريكيـة عـام 1981م؛ وهـي الفتـرة التـي تزامنـت مـع التحـول العمراني الواسـع الـذي شـهدته مدينة الرياض، حيـث أدى اعتمـاد المخطط العـام للمدينة فـي أواخر السـتينيات إلى انتشـار البيوت الحديثـة والمنـازل الخرسـانية. ورغم الحفـاظ علـى العديـد مـن المناطـق التاريخيـة، إلا أن هـذا المخطط أسـفر عـن تغييـرات عميقة في المشـهد العمراني للمدينة وتراثها المعماري.[1] ما أدى إلى إعادة تصنيف بيوت الطيـن في الوعي الجمعي،

Having grown up in a mud house, Alresayes experienced these structures firsthand, and he drew upon this knowledge in his later artistic practice, one deeply rooted in his upbringing in Najd. His family, active in the construction business, was among the first to adopt concrete construction. This made him acutely aware of the rapid urban modernization shaping the region. Traditional mud houses, crafted from raw earth mixed with straw and water,[2] have defined the Najd landscape for centuries. With their thick mud-covered walls, wooden doors and windows, and geometric motifs, these homes reflect a harmonious relationship with the surrounding environment, which Alresayes captures and reinterprets in his work.

In the 1980s, there was a growing awareness of the importance of preserving traditional culture, exemplified by events such as the Janadriyah festival, which promoted Saudi heritage. This period was defined by a dynamic relationship between architecture and community, and it highlighted how our built environment and identity shape one another. During this time, Alresayes, despite being far from home, initiated his Najdi-inspired architectural bodies of work that persisted throughout his career, taking shape as *Architectural Shapes*, *Architectural Elements*, and *Architectural Compositions*. These works navigate various levels of abstraction—some feature subtle geometric manipulations of entire buildings, while others present highly simplified outlines of architectural elements. Central to this exploration is Alresayes's focus on the traditional homes of Saudi Arabia, specifically their courtyards, facades, and distinctive features such as windows, arches, and decorative motifs.

Courtyards, in particular, embody the social and cultural values of these homes, acting as transitional spaces between public and private life, and

مـن كونها مجرد «بيوت عادية» إلـى أن أصبحت رمزاً للهوية «التقليدية»، ما عكس تحولاً عميقاً في نظرة المجتمــع لتراثـه العمراني.

نشأ محمد الرصيص في أحد البيـوت النجدية القديمة المبنية من الطين، الأمر الذي أتاح له مستقبلاً اختبار هذا الطراز من المباني شخصياً؛ واستعان بهذه المعرفة في ممارسته الفنية اللاحقة المتجذرة بعمق فـي نشـأته فـي نجـد؛ كمـا أن عائلته التـي عملت في مجـال البنـاء، كانـت مـن أوائل مـن تبنوا اسـتخدام الخرسـانة، ما جعله مـدركاً تماماً للتحديـث العمراني السـريع الذي أعاد تشـكيل منطقته، فلمئات السنين، تشكّل المشـهد العمراني في نجد من بيـوت الطين التقليديـة المبنية من التراب الممـزوج بالتبن والماء[2]، والتي عكسـت انسـجاماً فريداً مع البيئـة المحيطة، بجدرانها السميكة المغطاة بالطين، وأبوابها ونوافذها الخشـبية، وزخارفها الهندسـية، ليلتقـط الفنان هذه العلاقة المتناغمة ويعيد تشـكيلها في لوحاته.

فـي ثمانينيـات القـرن العشـرين، ازداد الوعـي بأهميـة الحفـاظ علـى الثقافـة التقليديـة، وتجسّـد ذلك في العديد من الفعاليـات التي احتفت بالتراث السـعودي، مثل مهرجـان الجنادرية. وشـهدت تلك الفترة تفاعـلاً ديناميكيـاً بين العمـارة والمجتمع، ما عكس العلاقة العميقة بيـن البيئة العمرانية والهوية الثقافيـة والاجتماعيـة في تلـك الأثناء، وعلـى الرغم من بُعده عن الوطن، بدأ الرصيص في رسـم لوحاته المعماريـة المسـتوحاة من العمـارة النجديـة، وهو توجهٌ استمر في تبنّيه طوال مسيرته الفنية. وجاءت أعمالـه تحـت عناويـن مختلفـة: «أشـكال معمارية» و«عناصـر معماريـة» و«تكوينـات معماريـة» وتتنقل هذه اللوحات بين مستويات مختلفة من التجريد؛ إذ يتميز بعضها بتلاعب هندسي دقيق بأشكال المباني، بينمـا يتضمـن البعـض الآخـر مخططات مبسطة للعناصر المعمارية، ويتجلى جوهر هذا الاستكشـاف في تركيز الرصيص على البيوت التقليدية في المملكة العربيـة السـعودية، ولا سـيما أفنيتهـا وواجهاتهـا وعناصرهـا المعماريـة المميـزة كالنوافـذ والأقـواس والزخـارف، والتي أصبحت سـمة بارزة فـي أعماله.

reflecting the fabric of Saudi society.[3] In the artist's abstractions, these spatial hierarchies become fluid, as Alresayes overlaps different areas of the home, exposing its core and revealing the sanctity of the courtyard. He also often depicts *shurfat*—distinctive battlements with rhythmic triangular or arrow-shaped patterns that crown the facades of these homes[4]—creating a visual dialogue between solid and void. In some works, these abstract elements evoke human silhouettes that emphasize the deep connection between the mud homes themselves and the people who inhabit them.

Alresayes also portrays cultural heritage through scenes of traditional and everyday activities in rural and Bedouin life. These works often depict individuals engaged in practices such as Qur'anic recitation, drumming, and dancing—moments deeply rooted in local culture. The figures are frequently rendered with distorted yet highly expressive facial features, recalling the influence of Pablo Picasso's Cubist phase. While Alresayes's early experiments with Cubist techniques were brief, their impact endures in his work, particularly in his treatment of perspective as well as his method of flattening three-dimensional space. Rather than adopting Cubism's simultaneous multiple viewpoints, Alresayes developed his own distinctive style that simplifies and flattens forms while maintaining their emotional resonance. Despite these Western influences, his work remains embedded in local cultural expression, capturing both the external representations of rural life, and the internal, emotional expressions of individuals. These scenes are often set within an architectural framework, whether prominently or indirectly, and structural surroundings peek out from behind the figures, subtly echoing his architectural bodies of work. Alresayes's geometric and spatial treatment of both figures and structures

يمكـن النظـر إلـى فنـاء البيـوت التقليديـة -بطن الحـوي- على أنها تجسـيد للقيم الاجتماعية والثقافية السـائدة، من حيث إنها تشكِّل مساحات انتقاليـة بين الحيـاة العامة والخاصة، عاكسـةً بذلك بنية المجتمع السعودي ونسيجه؛[3] غير أن الرصيص أزال عـن لوحاتـه الحـدود بيـن هـذه التقسـيمات المكانيـة، بحيـث تتداخل مختلف مساحات البيت علـى نحو يُظهر جوهره ويكشـف السـتار عن البُعد الرمـزي للفنـاء؛ كمـا أولـى الفنـان اهتمامـاً خاصـاً للشـرفات التـي تتـوج واجهـات البيـوت[4] وتعلوهـا الأنمـاط الهرميـة فـي حـوار بصـري بيـن الامتـلاء والفراغ. وفي بعض اللوحـات، تتحول هذه العناصر التجريديـة إلـى أشـكال أقرب ما تكون إلى صور البشر، مؤكدةً بذلك علـى الارتبـاط الوثيـق بيـن البيوت الطينية وسـاكنيها.

يعبّر الرصيـص عن التـراث الثقافي من خلال مشـاهده التي تصـور الأنشـطة التقليديـة واليومية فـي الحيـاة الريفيـة والبدويـة، حيـث يظهـر الناس في لوحاتـه وهم يتلـون القرآن، ويقرعـون الطبول أو يـؤدون الرقصات التراثية؛ وهـي لحظات متجذرة بعمـق فـي الثقافة المحليـة، وتبـدو شـخصياته بملامـح ملتويـة، ولكنهـا معبّـرة، كاشـفةً عـن تأثـر الفنان بالمرحلـة التكعيبية لدى بابلو بيكاسـو. ورغم أن تجاربـه الفنيـة المبكـرة مـع الأسـلوب التكعيبي كانـت وجيـزة، إلا أن تأثيرها ظل حاضـراً في أعماله، لا سـيما في معالجتـه للمنظور وتسـطيح الفضاء ثلاثـي الأبعـاد. ولكـن بـدلاً مـن تبنـي تعـدد زوايا الرؤيـة المتزامنـة كمـا فـي التكعيبيـة، طـور الفنان أسـلوبه الخـاص الذي يبسّـط الأشـكال ويسـطّحها مـع الحفاظ علـى توهّجهـا العاطفي، وعلـى الرغم من هـذه التأثيـرات الغربيـة، تبقى أعمـال الرصيص جزءًا لا يتجزأ مـن التعبير الثقافي المحلي، إذ تجمع بيـن التمثيلات الخارجيـة للحياة الريفية والتجليات الوجدانيـة العميقـة للنـاس، وغالبـاً مـا تتخذ هذه المشـاهد إطاراً معمارياً سواءً واضحاً أو ضمنياً، حيث تظهر المباني في خلفية الشـخصيات، مرددة صدى لوحات الفنان المعمارية. وبهذا تعزز هذه المعالجة

reinforces the intrinsic connection between people and their built environments.

Across both his architectural subjects and figurative work, Alresayes maintains a consistent artistic approach regardless of the subject matter. His distinctive style reduces the spatial depth of three-dimensional spaces and scenes with a flattened perception, integrating foreground and background into a leveled plane. While this flattening effect recalls Cubist innovations, his personal technique has evolved beyond these origins. In some works, he employs subtle depth cues through curved and angled lines, suggesting minimal perspective. Through the repetition of angular shapes and uninterrupted lines that segment the canvas into blocks of color, he brings a rhythmic nature into his work. Alresayes's color palette has therefore become a defining feature of his practice, reflecting both modernist influences and personal innovation. While his geometric forms show Cubist heritage, his approach to color reveals a thoughtful engagement with Impressionist principles. Like the Impressionists, who revolutionized painting by capturing the changing effects of light rather than local color, Alresayes moves beyond literal representation. However, where Impressionists sought to capture specific moments of natural light, Alresayes uses color more expressively and abstractly. Rather than adhering to the actual colors of a scene and the muted tones of mud houses, Alresayes infuses his compositions with light pastels and vivid hues. His bold use of reds, blues, and purples brings a sense of energy and playfulness to his compositions. Through this method, Alresayes breaks from academic conventions, reimagines spaces and scenes, and offers a unique perspective that blends traditional cultural heritage with personal interpretation.

الهندسـية والمكانيـة للشـخصيات والمبانـي فكـرة الارتبـاط الجوهـري بين الإنسـان وبيئتـه العمرانية.

وعلـى خطـوط متوازيـة فـي موضوعاتـه المعماريـة وأعمالـه التصويرية، يحافـظ محمـد الرصيـص علـى المقاربـة الفنيـة ذاتها بغـض النظر عـن الموضـوع، متبنّيـاً أسـلوباً يقلّـل مـن العمـق المكانـي ويسـطّح المسـاحات والمشـاهد ثلاثيـة الأبعـاد عبـر دمـج المقدمـة والخلفية في سـطح واحد. يذكّرنا هذا التسـطيح بالابتـكارات التكعيبية، إلاّ أن الفنـان طـور أسـلوبه الشـخصي إلـى مـا هو أبعـد مـن هـذه المرجعيات. ففـي بعـض أعماله، يوظف إشـارات عمـق دقيقة من خـلال الخطوط المنحنيـة والحـادة، مـا يعطـي الانطبـاع بوجـود المنظور ولو كان مبسـطاً. كما أن مـا يضفي إيقاعاً بصريـاً على العمـل الفني هو تكرار الأشـكال الحادة والخطـوط المتواصلـة التي تقسـم قمـاش اللوحة إلى كتـل مـن الألوان.

ومـن هنا، تصبـح الألـوان عنصـراً جوهرياً في تجربتـه الفنيـة؛ تعكس التأثيـرات الحداثيـة والرؤية الشـخصية في الآن نفسـه، وبينما تكشـف الأشكال الهندسية عن تأثر الرصيص بالتكعيبية، إلاّ أن مقاربته اللونيـة تعكس انخراطه المدروس فـي مبادئ التيار الانطباعـي. فعلـى غـرار الانطباعيين الذيـن أحدثوا ثـورة في عالم الرسـم من خـلال التقاطهـم تأثيرات الضـوء المتغيـرة بدلاً مـن اللون بحد ذاتـه؛ يتجاوز الرصيـص عتبة الرسـم المألوف في الفـن الانطباعـي الذي يسـعى إلى التقاط لحظـات معينة من الضوء الطبيعي، فهو يسـتخدم اللون بشـكل أكثر تعبيريةً وتجريداً، وعوضاً عن التزامه بألوان المشـهد الفعلية وتدرجـات بيـوت الطين الخافتـة، يلجأ إلـى الألوان الفاتحة والتدرجات الزاهية، مستخدماً ألواناً كالأحمر والأزرق والأرجواني بجرأة تضفي على أعماله شعوراً بالطاقة والمرح. وبهذه الطريقـة، يتحرّر الفنان من القواعد الأكاديمية الصارمة، ليعيد تصوّر المسـاحات والمشـاهد، مقدماً رؤيـة فريـدة يمـزج فيهـا بيـن التـراث الثقافي التقليدي وتأويله الشـخصي.

Between Forms explores the dual relationship between individuals and architecture in Alresayes's work. While his architectural and cultural scenes stand independently, they share connections: humans exist within the architecture, explicitly depicted or not, while figures take on architectural qualities. By choosing to depict mud homes, the artist represents these spaces that are imbued with social and cultural values. Constructed from earth and wood—living materials—these structures are more than mere forms; they are dynamic entities that breathe alongside society. Their angular forms, layered compositions, and vibrant colors serve as a rich visual vocabulary of Saudi legacy. By portraying architecture as a dynamic entity rather than a static one, the artist conveys these spaces as integral to society, both shaped by and shaping the people who inhabit them. Alresayes's depictions of traditional and local acts with an architectural lens reinforces the idea that we are deeply intertwined with our built environment, which forms an essential part of our lives.

يستكشـف معـرض «بيـن الطـراز» العلاقـة المزدوجـة بيـن الإنسـان والعمارة فـي أعمال محمد الرصيص، حيث تتمتع مشاهده المعمارية والثقافية باسـتقلاليتها، ولكنهـا تظـل دومـاً على صلـة وثيقة بالإنسـان، وتتجلـى هـذه الصلـة مـن خـلال وجود الشـخصيات ضمن هذه المشـاهد، بشـكل صريح أو ضمنـي، أو عبر تصوير البشـر بملامـح معمارية. وقد أراد الفنان من وراء اختيـاره لتصوير البيوت الطينية، تمثيل هذه المسـاحات المشـبعة بالقيم الاجتماعية والثقافيـة، باعتبارهـا أكثر من مجرد هيـاكل جامدة، بل كيانـات حيـة مبنية بالمـواد الطبيعيـة، كالطين والخشـب؛ تتنفـس وتتفاعـل مـع نبـض المجتمع، وتتجسـد هذه الرؤية عبر الأشـكال الحادة والتراكيب الطبقية والألوان الحيوية التي تحمل في طياتها إرثاً بصرياً سـعودياً غنياً. لم يكن الرصيص مهتماً بتصوير العمارة ككيان ثابت، بل كفضاء ديناميكي نابض يؤثر فـي سـاكنيه ويتأثر بهـم. ومن هـذا المنظـور، يعزز تصويره للأنشـطة التقليدية والمحليـة، مـن خلال عدسـة العمـارة، ومـن مُنطلـق الفكـرة القائلـة بأن الإنسـان وبيئتـه العمرانية فـي حالة تفاعل مسـتمر؛ فالمسـاحات المعمارية ليسـت مجرد خلفية للحياة اليوميـة، بل هي جزء جوهـري من الهويـة الثقافية، تعكـس وتشـكّل فـي الوقـت ذاتـه حيـاة المجتمـع وممارسـاته وقيمه.

1   Mohammed Alnaim, "The Typology of Courtyard Space in Najdi Architecture, Saudi Arabia: A Response to Human Needs, Culture, and the Environment," *Journal of Asian Architecture and Building Engineering* 23 (2023): 2.
2   Ali Saleh Al-Anbar, "A Study of the Interiors and Their Decoration in the Traditional Mud-Brick Architecture of the Najd Region of Saudi Arabia and the Factors That Have Influenced the Development of Interior Decoration and Spatial Organization" (PhD diss., Edinburgh College of Art, 1999), 43.
3   Mohammed Alnaim, "The Typology of Courtyard Space in Najdi Architecture, Saudi Arabia: A Response to Human Needs, Culture, and the Environment," *Journal of Asian Architecture and Building Engineering* 23 (2023): 2.
4   Latifa Al-Obailan and Abeer Alawad, "The Architectural Values Behind the Formation of Heritage Houses as a Tool for Promoting Cultural Identity in Saudi Arabia," Islamic Heritage Architecture IV (2022): 30.

1   محمد النعيم، «أنواع الأفنية في العمارة النجدية بالمملكة العربية السـعودية: اسـتجابة للاحتياجات الإنسانية والثقافية والبيئة»، مجلة العمارة وهندسـة البناء الآسيوية، (2023): 2.
2   علي صالح العنبر، «دراسـة الديكـورات الداخلية وزخارفها فـي عمارة الطوب اللبـن التقليدية بمنطقة نجد بالمملكة العربية السـعودية والعوامل المؤثرة فـي تطور الديكـور الداخلي والتنظيم المكاني» (رسـالة دكتـوراه، كلية إدنبره للفنون، 1999)، 43.
3   محمد النعيـم، «أنـواع الأفنيـة فـي العمـارة النجديـة بالمملكة العربيـة السعودية: اسـتجابة للاحتياجات الإنسانية والثقافية والبيئة»، مجلة العمارة وهندسة البناء الآسيوية، 23 (2023): 2.
4   لطيفة العبيلان وعبير العوض، «القيم المعمارية وراء تشـكيل البيوت التراثية كأداة لتعزيـز الهويـة الثقافيـة فـي المملكة العربيـة السـعودية»، العمـارة الإسلامية التراثية الرابع، 30 :(2022) IV.

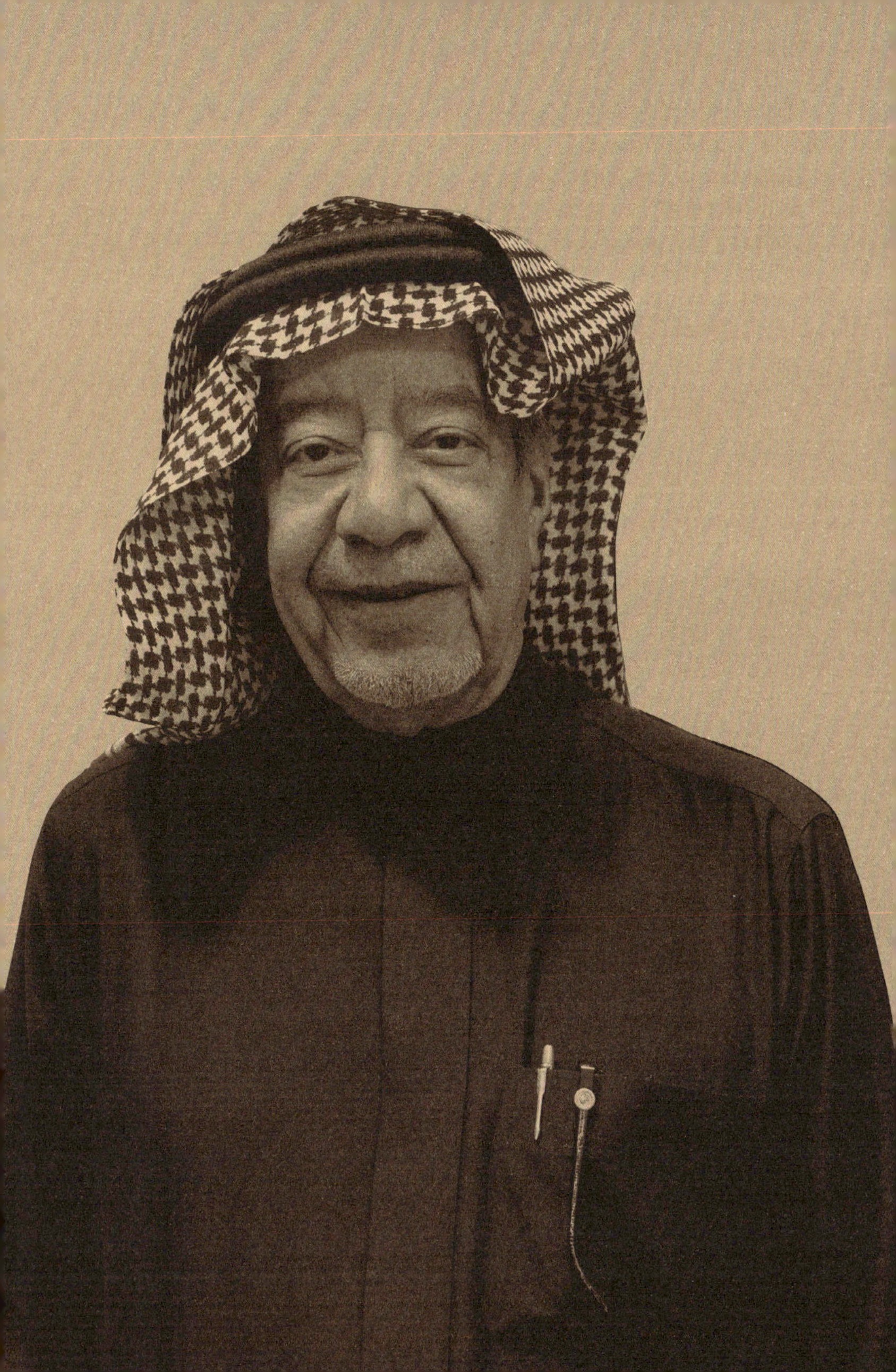

محمد الرصيّص
Mohammed Alresayes

مواليد 1951م في الرياض، المملكة العربية السعودية
b. 1951, Riyadh, Saudi Arabia

آرام العجاجي وندى العرادي
Aram Alajaji and Nada Alaradi

Painter, educator, writer, and art critic Mohammed Alresayes is distinguished by his abstractions of local and traditional Najdi architecture as well as his invaluable contributions to documenting Saudi art history through his critical writings. These accomplishments have established him as a key figure in the country's cultural landscape. Throughout his career, Alresayes has cultivated a distinct aesthetic that blends abstract and modernist trends while drawing inspiration from Saudi heritage.

In 1969, Alresayes was part of the second graduating class from the Institute of Art Education in Riyadh. There, he studied under Iraqi artist and educator Saadi Alkaabi (b. 1937), whose practice involved taking his students to sketch around the neighborhoods in Riyadh and Diriyah. This left a profound impact on Alresayes, as it ignited his fascination with architecture. After completing his studies, he served as a teaching assistant at the Institute of Art Education from 1971 to 1973, and he worked as an assistant lecturer at King Saud University in the Department of Art Education in 1977 after earning a bachelor's degree in Art Education (Fine Arts) from Helwan University, Egypt (1977).

محمـد الرصيّص رسّـامٌ ومعلـم وكاتـب وناقد فني، يتميّـز بإبداعاتـه التجريديـة التـي تعكـس جماليات العمارة النجديـة المحلية والتقليدية، وقد ترك من خلال كتاباته النقديـة القيّمة بصمةٌ عميقة في توثيق تاريـخ الفـن السـعودي، ما رسّـخ مكانته كشخصيةٍ رائدة في المشـهد الثقافـي الوطني. نجح على مدى مسـيرته الفنية فـي تطوير رؤيـة جماليـة تمزج بين اتجاهات المدرسـة التجريدية، مسـتلهمةً من عراقة التراث السـعودي.

فـي عـام 1969م، كان الرصيّـص مـن خريجي الدفعـة الثانيـة في معهـد التربية الفنيـة للمعلمين بالريـاض، حيـث تتلمـذ علـى يـد الفنـان والمـدرّس العراقي سعدي الكعبي الذي اعتاد اصطحابَ طلّابه لرسم المشاهد المستوحاة من المباني التاريخية في أحيـاء الرياض والدرعية، ما ترك أثراً عميقاً في نفس الرصيّـص وأوقد شـغفه بفن العمـارة. بعد تخرجه، بـدأ مسـيرته المهنيـة كمعلّم مسـاعد فـي معهد التربيـة الفنيـة من عـام 1971م حتى عـام 1973م، ثـم انتقـل ليشـغل منصـب معيـد بقسـم التربيـة الفنية في جامعة الملك سـعود عـام 1977م، بعد حصولـه على درجـة البكالوريوس فـي التربية الفنية (تصويـر تشـكيلي) مـن جامعة حلـوان بمصر عام 1977م، ثم واصل مسيرته الأكاديمية بحصوله على درجة الماجسـتير في الفنون (تصوير تشـكيلي) من

Alresayes then pursued several degrees: a Master of Fine Arts from Ohio State University, USA (1982); and a PhD in Art Education (Museum Education) from Ohio State University, USA (1989). His doctoral thesis, "The importance of the emergence and development of museums of art and traditional crafts in the Kingdom of Saudi Arabia," focused on the country's arts sector. His commitment to fostering the development of art education within the Saudi community extended beyond borders—in 1986, while in the United States, he and his colleagues cofounded the Saudi Society for Art Education in America.

The artist returned to Saudi Arabia in 1989 and worked as an assistant professor in Art Education at King Saud University's College of Education in Riyadh. Over the course of eighteen years, he made significant contributions to the institution, including a six-year tenure as head of the Department of Art Education from 1992 to 1997. Following his retirement in 2006, Alresayes took on leadership roles at the Saudi Arabian Society for Culture and Arts, serving as its secretary of the board of directors for five years and later as chairman.

Alresayes's artistic practice and technique evolved significantly over the decades. During his time in Egypt, he studied Impressionist art, aiming to merge its signature brushstrokes with the fragmented, reassembled spaces of Cubism. In the 1980s, his work frequently depicted rural scenes in Saudi Arabia, including Bedouin and village life on farms and in deserts. Encouraged by his teachers, Alresayes explored diverse themes, producing series such as *Small Creatures*, which focused on insects and birds. Other abstract works examined shape, form, and negative space, along with architectural compositions that later became central to his oeuvre. During the same decade, he delved into themes of famine and

جامعــة ولايــة أوهايــو بالولايـات المتحـدة الأمريكيـة عـام 1982م، ودرجــة الدكتـوراه فـي التربيـة الفنيـة (تربيـة متحفية) مـن نفـس الجامعـة عام 1989م، وقـد كانت رسـالته للدكتـوراه بعنـوان: «أهمية نشـوء وتطـور متاحـف الفـن والصناعـات التقليديـة فـي المملكة العربية السـعودية» والتي ركزت على توثيق تطـور القطـاع الفنـي فـي المملكة؛ أثناء دراسـته في الولايـات المتحـدة. وفي عـام 1986م، شـارك فـي تأسـيس الجمعية السـعودية للتربية الفنية بأمريكا، مواصـلاً تفانيـه فـي تطويـر مجـال التربيـة الفنيـة، سـواء داخـل المملكـة أو خارجهـا.

عـاد محمـد الرصيّـص إلـى المملكـة العربيـة السـعودية فـي عـام 1989م ليبدأ مسـيرةً أكاديمية جديـدة كأسـتاذ مسـاعد فـي قسـم التربيـة الفنيـة بكليـة التربية بجامعة الملك سـعود بالرياض، وعلى مدار ثمانية عشـر عامـاً، قدم إسـهامات كبيرة للكلية، حيـث شـغل منصب رئيس القسـم لمدة ستة أعوام، مـن عـام 1992م حتى عـام 1997م وبعـد تقاعده فـي عـام 2006م، تولى أدواراً قياديـة في الجمعية العربية السعودية للثقافة والفنون، حيـث عمل أميناً لمجلس الإدارة لمـدة خمسـة أعوام قبـل أن يتقلّد منصب رئيـس المجلس.

تطور أسـلوب الرصيّص وتقنياتـه الفنية تطوراً لافتاً على مـرّ العقود المنصرمة، وكان قد درس الفن الانطباعـي الـذي يتميـز بضربات الفرشـاة السـريعة أثنـاء فترة إقامتـه في مصـر، وعمل علـى مزجه مع الأسـلوب التكعيبي الذي يقوم على تفكيك مساحات الرسـم وإعـادة تركيبهـا، فـي الثمانينيات مـن القرن العشـرين وتميّـزت أعماله آنـذاك بتصوير المشـاهد الريفيـة وأنماط الحيـاة البدويـة والقروية في المزارع والصحاري في المملكة العربية السـعودية، وبتشـجيع من أسـاتذته، انطلق في استكشاف موضوعات فنية متنوعـة، بدءاً من سلسـلة «الكائنـات الصغيرة» التي تنـاول فيهـا الحشـرات والطيـور، وصـولاً إلـى أعماله التجريدية التي اسـتعرض فيها الشـكل والفـراغ، إلى جانـب التكوينات المعمارية التـي أصبحت فيما بعد سـمةً مميزة لهويته الفنية.

human suffering, creating emotionally charged works. Some of his paintings take on a darker, more enigmatic quality, characterized by dense layers of paint and the introduction of a figurative style that challenged the conventions of the Saudi art scene. In the 1990s, Alresayes engaged with the emerging Expressionist movement through numerous large-scale paintings that addressed themes of exile, pain, and misery.

The artist's practice is deeply rooted in Saudi national heritage, a connection he began to explore during his postgraduate studies in the United States, where feelings of nostalgia and longing for his culture profoundly influenced his work. This exploration took form through several bodies of work, including *Architectural Shapes, Architectural Elements,* and *Architectural Composition.* These works were derived from the design of traditional clay houses, and sequentially, they became increasingly abstract as the source of inspiration became more ambiguous; he has described this as "abstract and minimalist expressionism." As rooms overlap, the artist deconstructs his inspiration into shapes and elements, playing with proportion, color, and perspective, particularly in his renowned series *Architectural Elements.* In such works, Alresayes draws from Islamic and folk art, deconstructing architectural elements into windows, balconies, doors, and decorative motifs. These works represent a pivotal development in his artistic journey, which he continues to revisit.

Alresayes held four solo exhibitions, including at Alnassr Club F. C., Riyadh, Saudi Arabia (1972); in Columbus, Ohio (1982); *Civilizational Symbols,* Saudi Art House, Riyadh, Saudi Arabia (1983); and a retrospective exhibition at the National Museum, in King Abdulaziz Historical Center, Riyadh, Saudi Arabia (2002). He began participating in local group exhibitions in 1973, including those organized by the

تعمّـق الرصيـص فـي نفـس العقـد فـي تقصّي موضوعـات المجاعـة والمآسـي الإنسـانية، الأمر الذي أثمـر أعمـالاً تحمل شـحنة عاطفيـة هائلـة وتميزت بعض لوحاته خلال تلك الفترة بسوداويتها وغموضها، حيث اعتمد علـى طبقـات الطلاء الكثيفة والأسـلوب التشـخيصي المغاير لما كان سائداً في المشهد الفني السـعودي. وسـرعان ما انخرط في الحركـة التعبيرية الناشـئة فـي تسـعينيات القرن العشـرين، حيث قدّم العديد مـن اللوحـات كبيـرة الحجـم التـي تناولـت موضوعـات المنفـى والألم والبؤس الإنسـاني.

يتجـذّر فـن محمـد الرصيّـص تجـذّراً عميقـاً فـي التـراث الوطنـي السـعودي، إذ ظهـرت ملامح هـذا التجـذر التراثـي أثنـاء دراسـته للماجسـتير فـي الولايـات المتحـدة؛ حينهـا تأثرت أعمالـه الفنية تأثراً بالغـاً بحنينـه لوطنـه وشـوقه لثقافته، مـا انعكس فـي عـدد مـن المجموعـات المميّـزة مثل «أشـكال معمارية» و«عناصـر معمارية» و«تكوينات معمارية»، والمسـتمدة من تصاميم المنـازل الطينية التقليدية، غيـر أن أسـلوب الفنـان أصبـح مـع مرور الوقـت أكثر تجريديـةً مـع تزايـد غموض مصـادر إلهامـه، وقد وصف الرصيص أسلوبه في تلك المرحلة «بالتعبيرية التجريدية والتبسيطية»، وراح في تفكيك نماذجه إلى أشـكال وعناصر، متلاعباً بالنسـب والألوان والمنظور، وخاصـة فـي سلسـلته الشـهيرة «عناصـر معمارية»، حيث اسـتقى من الفن الإسـلامي والشـعبي، مفكّكاً العناصـر المعماريـة إلـى نوافـذ وشـرفات وأبـواب وأنماط زخرفية، وبهذا شـكّلت هذه السلسـلة نقطة تحـوّل فارقة في مسـيرته الفنية، وهـو لا يزال يعود إلى ذلـك الأسـلوب المميز حتى اليوم.

أقام الرصيّـص أربعة معـارض فردية وشـملت معرضـاً في نـادي النصر بالريـاض، المملكـة العربية السـعودية (1972م)، ومعرضاً في كولومبيوس، أوهايو (1982م)، وآخر بعنوان «رموز حضارية» في دار الفنون السـعودية بالرياض (1983م)، ومعرضاً اسـتعادياً في المتحـف الوطنـي بمركز الملـك عبدالعزيـز التاريخي بالرياض، المملكـة العربيـة السـعودية (2002م). إلى جانب ذلك، كان له عدد من المشاركات في المعارض

Institute of Art Education, the General Presidency of Youth Welfare, and King Saud University in Riyadh. Alresayes's more recent group exhibitions include *Khamseen: 50 Years of Saudi Visual Arts*, Sotheby's, London, United Kingdom (2024); *Echoing the Land*, Prince Faisal bin Fahd Arts Hall, Riyadh, Saudi Arabia (2023); *After a While: "Al-Kaabi and His Students,"* Tuwaiq Palace, Riyadh, Saudi Arabia (2020); *Decades*, Mono Gallery, Riyadh, Saudi Arabia (2018); *Past Is Prologue*, 21,39, Saudi Art Council, Jeddah, Saudi Arabia (2014); and *Al Taliaa: The Beginnings of Fine Art in Saudi Arabia*, Hafez Gallery, Riyadh, Saudi Arabia (2014). His works have also been exhibited in Egypt, the United Kingdom, Turkey, Spain, France, Taiwan, and the United States. In addition to his exhibitions, Alresayes is an accomplished writer and art critic. He has written numerous articles for Saudi newspapers, such as *Al Eqtisadiah, Al Riyadh*, and *Aljazeera*, and published several books, including *Man and Plastic Arts* (1992, coauthored with Saleh Alzayer), *The 7th Janadriyah Plastic Arts* (1993, coauthored with Saleh Alzayer), *Plastic Arts in the Kingdom of Saudi Arabia* (2010), and *History of Plastic Arts in the Kingdom of Saudi Arabia* (2010). In addition, Alresayes has contributed extensively to the field of contemporary Saudi art through numerous art research papers.

Mohammed Alresayes has solidified himself as a pillar within the Saudi art community through his representation of local architecture, his scholarly contributions, and his commitment to fostering local artistic growth. His contributions as an artist, educator, and writer are a cornerstone of Saudi art history, and they will continue to shape the region's cultural dialogue, inspiring future generations to explore and be inspired by their heritage.

الجماعيــة المحليــة منذ عــام 1973م، بمــا فيها تلك التــي نظمهــا معهــد التربية الفنيــة والرئاســة العامة لرعاية الشباب وجامعة الملك سعود بالرياض، وتشمل أحدثُ مشــاركاته معرض «خمســون عاماً من الفنون البصرية الســعودية» في دار ســوثبي للمـزادات بلندن (2024م)، ومعــرض «مــن حولهم» فــي قاعة الأمير فيصل بن فهد للفنون بالريــاض (2023م)، ومعرض «بعــد حيــن - الكعبــي وتلاميــذه» فــي قصر طويق بالرياض (2020م)، ومعرض «عقود» في مونو جاليري بالرياض (2018م)، ومعرض «الماضي كمقدمة» ضمن مبــادرة فـن جـدة 21,39، بتنظيــم المجلس الفني الســعودي (2014م)، ومعــرض «الطليعــة: بدايـات الفن التشكيلي السعودي» في حافظ جاليري بالرياض (2014م). وامتدت مشــاركات الرصيص الفنية إلى دول عديدة، منها مصر والمملكة المتحدة وتركيا وإســبانيا وفرنســا وتايوان والولايات المتحدة.

علاوةً على نشــاطه الفني، يُعد محمد الرصيص مـن أبـرز الكتّـاب والنقّاد الفنييــن في المملكـة، حيث كتب عشــرات المقالات في الصحف الســعودية، مثل صحيفة «الاقتصاديـة» و«الرياض» و «الجزيـرة»، وألّف عـدداً مـن الكتب المهمـة، منهـا: «الفنون التشكيلية والإنسان» (1992م، بمشاركة د. صالح الزاير)، و«الفنون التشـكيلية في الجنادريـة 7» (1993م، أيضاً بمشـاركة د. صالح الزاير)، و«الفن التشــكيلي في المملكة العربية الســعودية» (2010م)، و«تاريـخ الفـن التشــكيلي في المملكـة العربيــة الســعودية» (2010م). كما أســهم بمقالات فنية متنوعـة أثرت المشــهد الفني المعاصر في المملكة وأســهمت فـي تطوره.

اســتطاع محمــد الرصيــص ترســيخ مكانته كأحد أعمـدة الفن الســعودي بفضل تمثيله البــارع للعمارة المحلية، وإسـهاماته العلمية الغنية، والتزامه الراسـخ بتطوير الفنـون المحلية، وشــكّلت أعمالَه وإســهاماته كفنان ومـدرّس وكاتب، حجز الأسـاس في بنـاء تاريخ الفن الســعودي، ما جعله رمزاً ثقافياً يواصل التأثير في المشهد الفني وفي صياغة الحوار الثقافي في المنطقة، لتظل إنجازاته مصدر إلهام للأجيال القادمة لاستكشاف التراث السعودي والنهل من روافده الغنيّة.

Mohammed Alresayes was born in Riyadh, Saudi Arabia	**1951**	وُلد محمد الرصيّص في الرياض بالمملكة العربية السعودية
Art was incorporated into the public school curriculum, and it was taught at every level throughout Saudi Arabia's general education system	**1957**	اعتمـاد تدريـس التربيـة الفنيـة في المناهج الدراسـية لجميع المسـتويات في المدارس الحكومية في نظـام التعليم العام في المملكة العربية السعودية
The Institute of Art Education was established in Riyadh, Saudi Arabia	**1965**	تأسـيس معهّد التربية الفنية للمعلمين في الرياض بالمملكة العربية السعودية
Alresayes obtained a diploma in art education for teachers from the Institute of Art Education in Riyadh, Saudi Arabia	**1969**	حصـل الرصيّص على دبلـوم معهد التربيـة الفنية للمعلمين بالرياض، المملكة العربية السعودية
Alresayes served as a teaching assistant at the Institute of Art Education in Riyadh, Saudi Arabia until 1973	**1971**	بدأ بالعمل كمعلّم مسـاعد في معهد التربية الفنية بالرياض، المملكة العربية السعودية حتى 1973م
Alresayes held his first solo exhibition at Alnassr Club F.C., Riyadh, Saudi Arabia	**1972**	افتتـح المعـرض الفـردي الأول للرصيـص فـي نـادي النصـر بالريـاض، المملكـة العربيـة السـعودية
The Saudi Arabian Society for Culture and Arts was established in Riyadh, and thirteen branches opened across Saudi Arabia in the following years	**1973**	تأسيس الجمعية العربية السعودية للثقافة والفنون بالرياض، وافتتاح ثلاثة عشر فرعاً لها في مختلف أنحـاء المملكة في الأعوام التالية
Alresayes began participating in local group exhibitions in Riyadh, Saudi Arabia		بدء مشـاركة الرصيّص في المعارض الجماعيـة المحلية في الرياض، المملكة العربية السعودية
The General Presidency of Youth Welfare was established as an independent governmental institution with a dedicated Fine Arts Department in Riyadh, Saudi Arabia	**1974**	تأسـيس الرئاسـة العامة لرعاية الشـباب كمؤسسـة حكومية مسـتقلة، مع قسـم تابع لها متخصص في الفنون التشكيلية في الريـاض، المملكة العربية السـعودية
Alresayes earned a bachelor's degree in art education (fine arts) from Helwan University in Cairo, Egypt	**1977**	حصـل الرصيّص علـى درجة البكالوريـوس في التربية الفنية (تصويـر تشـكيلي) من جامعـة حلوان بالقاهـرة، مصر
Alresayes worked as an assistant lecturer in the Department of Art Education at King Saud University in Riyadh, Saudi Arabia, until 1978		بـدأ بالعمـل كمعيـد فـي قسـم التربيـة الفنيـة بجامعـة الملـك سـعود بالريـاض، المملكـة العربية السـعودية حتى عـام 1978م
The Saudi Art House was established in Riyadh, Saudi Arabia, by Mohammed Alsaleem; the International Gallery, which exhibits works by both national and international artists, was later added	**1979**	تأسـيس دار الفنـون السـعودية علـى يـد محمـد السـليم فـي الريـاض، المملكة العربية السـعودية، والتـي أُضيفـت إليهـا لاحقـاً صالـة العـرض العالميـة التـي تسـتضيف الفنانين الوطنيين والعالميين
Alresayes completed a Master of Fine Arts from Ohio State University, USA, and held his second solo exhibition	**1982**	حصل الرصيص علـى درجة الماجسـتير في الفنـون (تصوير تشكيلي) من جامعة ولاية أوهايو بالولايات المتحدة وافتتح المعرضه الفردي الثاني.
Alresayes held his third solo exhibition, *Civilizational Symbols*, at Saudi Art House, Riyadh, Saudi Arabia	**1983**	افتتح المعرض الفردي الثالث للرصيص بعنوان «رموز حضارية» في دار الفنون السعودية بالرياض، المملكة العربية السعودية
Alresayes began publishing diverse art articles in the Saudi press		بداية نشره المقالات الفنية في الصحافة السعودية
Alresayes became a cofounding member of the Saudi Society for Art Education in America	**1986**	أصبـح عضوًا مؤسسـا للجمعيـة السـعودية للتربية الفنية فـي أمريكا
Alresayes received a PhD in art education (museum education) from Ohio State Univerisy, USA	**1989**	حصل الرصيص على درجة دكتوراه الفلسفة في مجال التربية الفنية (تربية متحفية) من جامعة أوهايو الحكومية، الولايات المتحدة الأمريكية

1989

Alresayes became a member and rapporteur of several academic committees at King Saud University in Riyadh, Saudi Arabia, until 2006

عضو ومقرر لعـدة لجان أكاديمية بجامعة الملك سـعود بالرياض، المملكة العربية السعودية

Alresayes became an assistant professor in the Department of Art Education at the College of Education, King Saud University

بدأ بالعمل كأستاذ مساعد بقسم التربية الفنية بكلية التربية بجامعة الملك سعود حتى 2006م

1992

Alresayes coauthored *Man and Plastic Arts* with Saleh Alzayer

تأليف كتاب «الفنون التشكيلية والإنسان» بمشاركة د. صالح الزاير

Alresayes served as the head of the Department of Art Education at King Saud University until 1997

بـدأ بالعمـل كرئيـس لقسم التربيـة الفنية بجامعـة الملك سـعود حتى 1997م

1993

Alresayes coauthored *The 7th Janadriyah Plastic Arts* with Saleh Alzaer

تأليـف كتاب «الفنون التشـكيلية فـي الجنادرية 7» بمشـاركة د. صالح الزاير

1997

Alresayes represented Saudi Arabia as an "observer" at the Congrés: Condition de l'artiste, UNESCO in Paris, France

مثّـل الرصيـص المملكـة بصفـة مراقـب فـي المؤتمـر الدولي الخـاص بعنـوان «وضـع الفنان» فـي باريس، فرنسـا

2002

Alresayes held his fourth solo exhibition, a retrospective, at the National Museum at King Abdulaziz Historical Center, Riyadh, Saudi Arabia

افتتـح المعرض الفردي الرابع معرضاً اسـتعادياً في المتحف الوطني بمركز الملـك عبد العزيز التاريخـي بالرياض، المملكة العربية السعودية

2003

Alresayes began to write and edit the weekly newspaper column "Plastic Art," which appeared in *Al Eqtisadiah* until 2005

بـدأ بالعمـل ككاتـب ومحـرر لصفحة «الفن التشكيلي» الأسـبوعية في صحيفة «الاقتصادية» حتى عام 2005م

Alresayes became a member of the Advisory Board for Culture at the Ministry of Culture and Information until 2005, and for a second time from 2009 until 2012

عضو في الهيئة الاستشـارية للثقافة بـوزارة الثقافة والإعلام حتـى عـام 2005، وفـي الفتـرة الثانيـة مـن 2009م الـى 2012م

2004

Alresayes participated as a member of the Saudi delegation to the Permanent Committee for Arab Media and Culture in Tunis, Tunisia

شارك في وفد المملكة في اجتماع اللجنة الدائمة للإعلام والثقافة العربية بتونس العاصمة، تونس

2006

Alresayes served as secretary of the Board of Directors of the Saudi Arabian Society for Culture and Arts until 2011

بـدأ بالعمـل كأميـن لمجلس الإدارة فـي الجمعيـة العربية السـعودية للثقافة والفنون حتـى عـام 2011م

2010

Alresayes authored *Plastic Arts in the Kingdom of Saudi Arabia*, published by the Arab League Educational, Cultural and Scientific Organization in Tunis, Tunisia

قـام بتأليـف كتـاب «الفـن التشـكيلي فـي المملكة العربية السـعودية» إصدار ونشـر المنظمـة العربية للتربيـة والثقافة والعلـوم بتونـس العاصمـة، تونس

Alresayes authored *History of Plastic Arts in the Kingdom of Saudi Arabia*, published by the Ministry of Culture and Information in Riyadh, Saudi Arabia; it was translated into Italian in 2015

قـام بتأليـف كتاب «تاريخ الفن التشكيلي في المملكة العربية السعودية» إصدار ونشر وزارة الثقافة والإعلام بالرياض، وتمت ترجمته إلى اللغة الإيطالية في عام 2015

2011

Alresayes was the Chairman of the Board of Directors of the Saudi Arabian Society for Culture and Arts until 2012

رئيس مجلس الإدارة في الجمعية العربية السعودية للثقافة والفنون حتى عام 2012م

2012

Alresayes was a committee member of the Ministry of Culture and Information Book Award until 2014

عضو في لجنـة جائـزة وزارة الثقافـة والإعلام للكتـاب حتى عام 2014م

2013

The Saudi Art Council was established in Jeddah, Saudi Arabia

تأسيس المجلس الفني السعودي بجدة، المملكة العربية السعودية

2014

Alresayes was featured in the group exhibition *Past Is Prologue*, as part of 21,39, organized by the Saudi Art Council, Jeddah, Saudi Arabia

شـارك فـي المعرض الجماعـي «الماضـي كمقدمـة» ضمـن مبادرة فـن حـدة 21,39، بتنظيم المجلـس الفني السـعودي

Hafez Gallery was founded in Jeddah, Saudi Arabia

تأسيس حافظ جاليري في جدة، المملكة العربية السعودية

Alresayes was featured in the group exhibition *Al Taliaa: The Beginnings of Fine Art in Saudi Arabia* at Hafez Gallery, Jeddah, Saudi Arabia

شـارك فـي المعرض الجماعـي «الطليعـة: بدايـات الفـن التشـكيلي السـعودي» فـي حافظ جاليـري بجـدة، المملكة العربيـة السـعودية

2017

Misk Art Institute was established in Riyadh, Saudi Arabia

تأسيس معهد مسك للفنون بالرياض، المملكة العربية السعودية

Mono Gallery was founded in Riyadh, Saudi Arabia

تأسيس مونو جاليري بالرياض، المملكة العربية السعودية

Alresayes was honored by Misk Art Institute as a pioneer in Saudi arts	**2018**	تكريمه من قبل معهد مسك للفنون باعتبـاره من كبار رواد الفن السعودي
Alresayes was featured in the group exhibition *Decades* at Mono Gallery, Riyadh, Saudi Arabia		شـــارك في المعـرض الجماعـي «عقـود» في مونـو جاليري بالريـاض، المملكـة العربية السـعودية
Alresayes was featured in the group exhibition *Space: A Tale*, organized by Misk Art Institute, at Prince Faisal bin Fahd Arts Hall, Riyadh, Saudi Arabia		شـــارك فـي المعـرض الجماعـي «حكايـة مكان» مـن تنظيم معهد مسـك للفنون، في صالة الأمير فيصل بن فهد للفنون بالرياض، المملكة العربية السـعودية
Alresayes was featured in the group exhibition *After a While: "Al-Kaabi and His Students"* at Tuwaiq Palace, Riyadh, Saudi Arabia	**2020**	شـــارك في المعرض الجماعي «بعد حين - الكعبي وتلاميذه» في قصر طويق بالرياض، المملكة العربية السعودية
Alresayes was featured in the group exhibition *Echoing the Land*, organized by Misk Art Institute, Riyadh, Saudi Arabia	**2023**	شـــارك فـي المعـرض الجماعـي «مـن حولهم» مـن تنظيم معهد مسـك للفنون، في صالة الأمير فيصل بن فهد للفنون بالرياض، المملكة العربية السـعودية
Alresayes was featured in the group exhibition *Khamseen: 50 Years of Saudi Visual Arts* at Sotheby's, London, United Kingdom	**2024**	شـــارك في المعـرض الجماعي «خمسـون عاماً مـن الفنون البصريـة السـعودية» فـي دار سـوثبي للمـزادات بلنـدن، المملكة المتحدة

الأعمال الفنية
Artworks

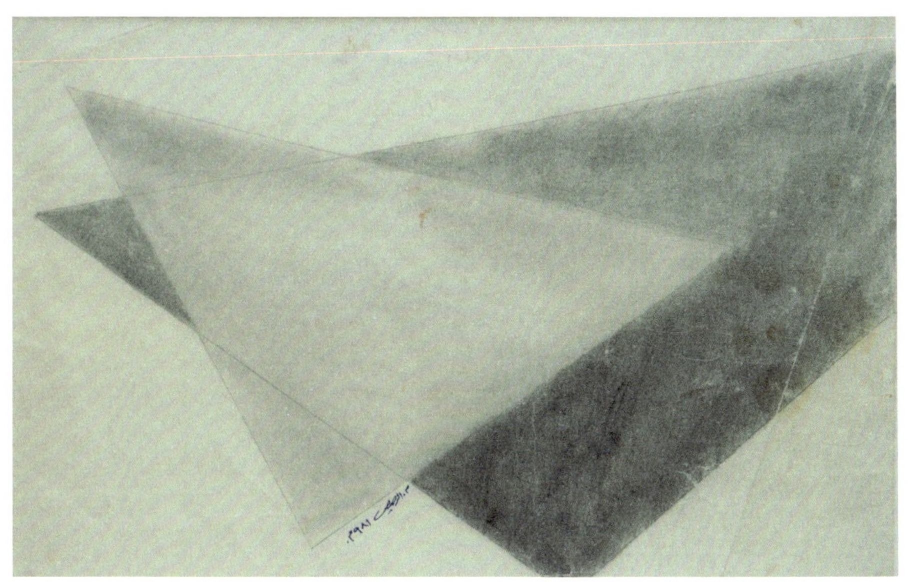

تخطيط أولي

دراسة هندسية، 1981

قلم رصاص على ورق
27.5 × 44.5 سم
بإذن من الفنان وإرم جاليري في الرياض

Architectural Studies,
preparatory drawing, 1981

Graphite on paper
27.5 × 44.5 cm
Courtesy of the artist and Errm Art Gallery in
Riyadh, Saudi Arabia

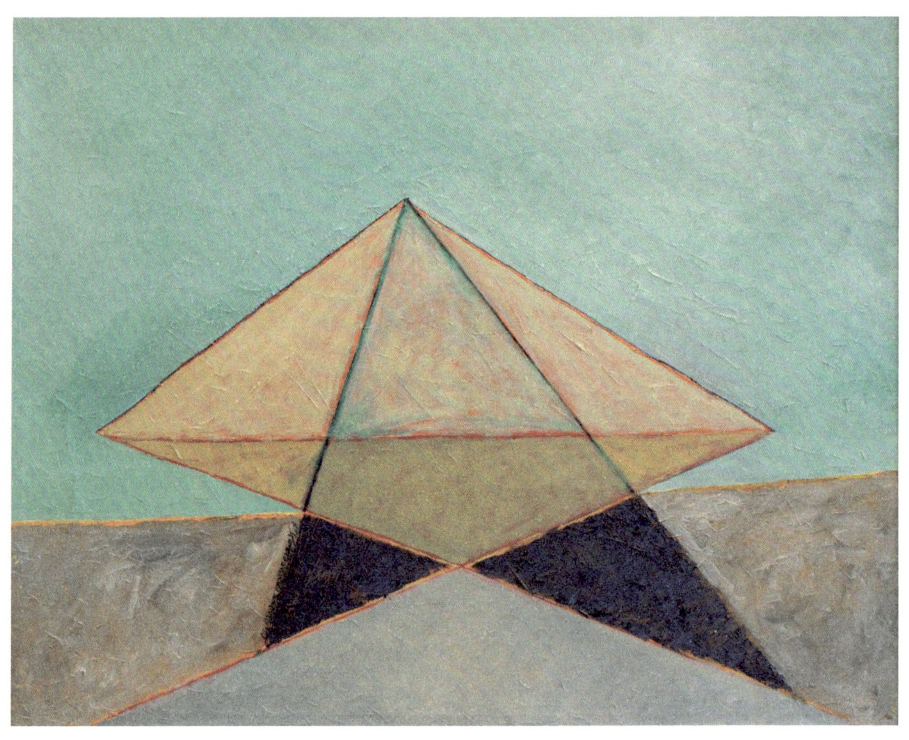

Architectural Elements 2, 1982

Oil on canvas
104.5 × 135 cm
Courtesy of the artist and Hewar Art Gallery in
Riyadh, Saudi Arabia

عناصر معمارية 2، 1982

ألوان زيتية على قماش
104.5 × 135 سم
بإذن من الفنان وحوار جاليري في الرياض

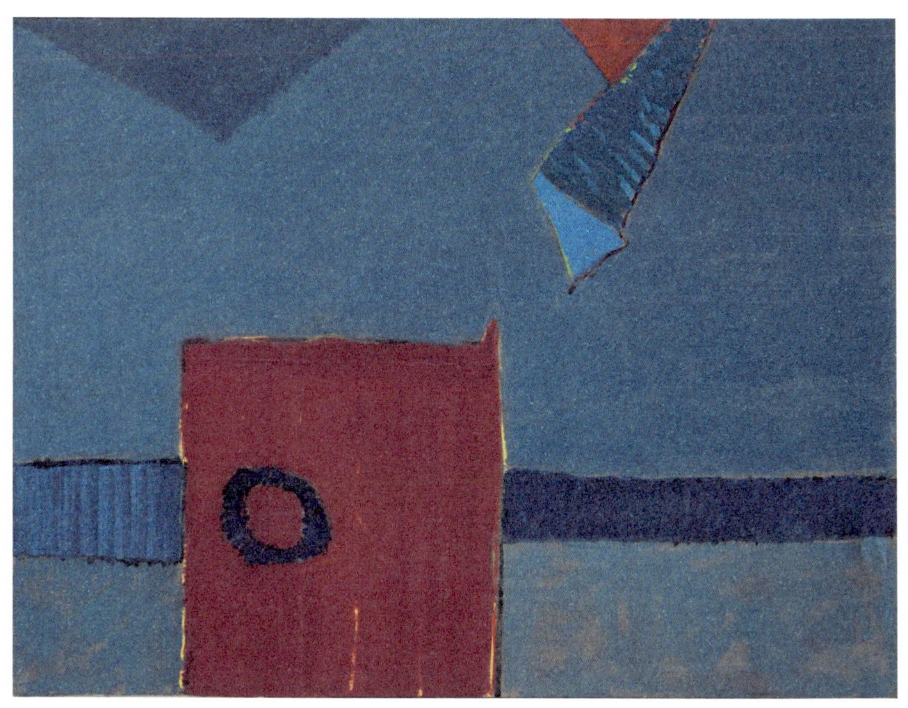

عناصر معمارية 3، 1982

ألوان زيتية على قماش
112 × 150 سم
بإذن من الفنان وحافظ جاليري في جده

Architectural Elements 3, 1982

Oil on canvas
112 × 150 cm
Courtesy of the artist and Hafez Gallery in Jeddah,
Saudi Arabia

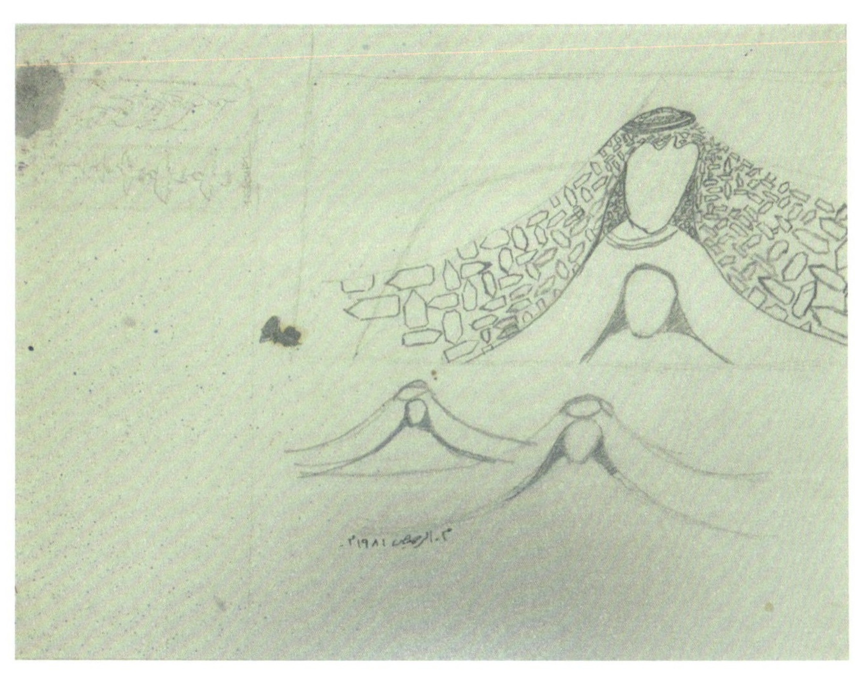

Shamagh,
preparatory drawing, 1981

Graphite on paper
21.5 × 29 cm
Courtesy of the artist and Errm Art Gallery in
Riyadh, Saudi Arabia

تخطيط أولي
لشماغ، 1981

قلم رصاص على ورق
21.5 × 29 سم
بإذن من الفنان وإرم جاليري في الرياض

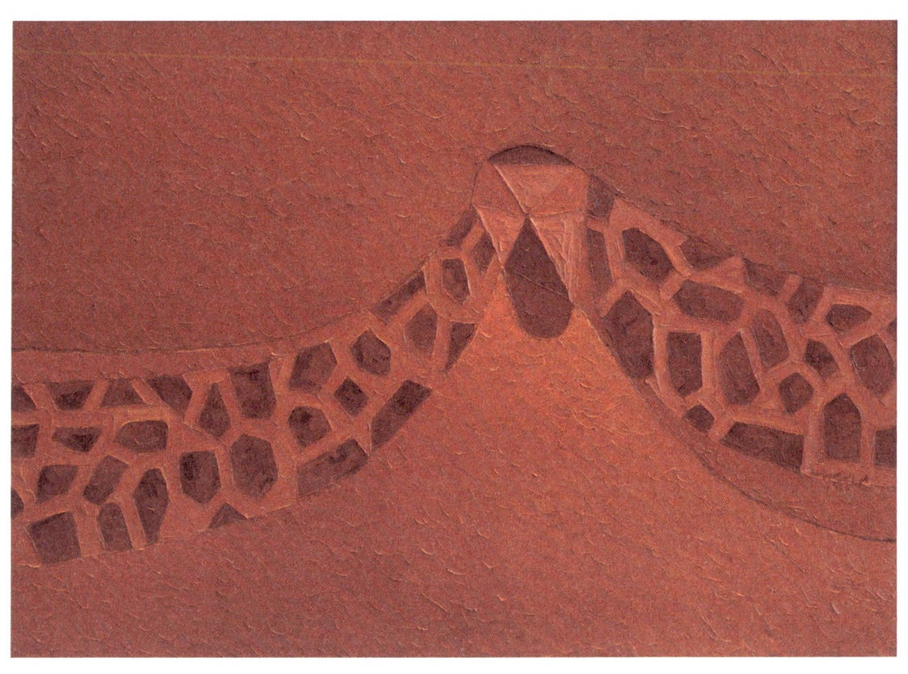

رأس بالشماغ، 1980

ألوان زيتية على قماش
88 × 126 سم
بإذن من الفنان وحوار جاليري في الرياض

Shamagh, 1980

Oil on canvas
88 × 126 cm
Courtesy of the artist and Hewar Art Gallery in
Riyadh, Saudi Arabia

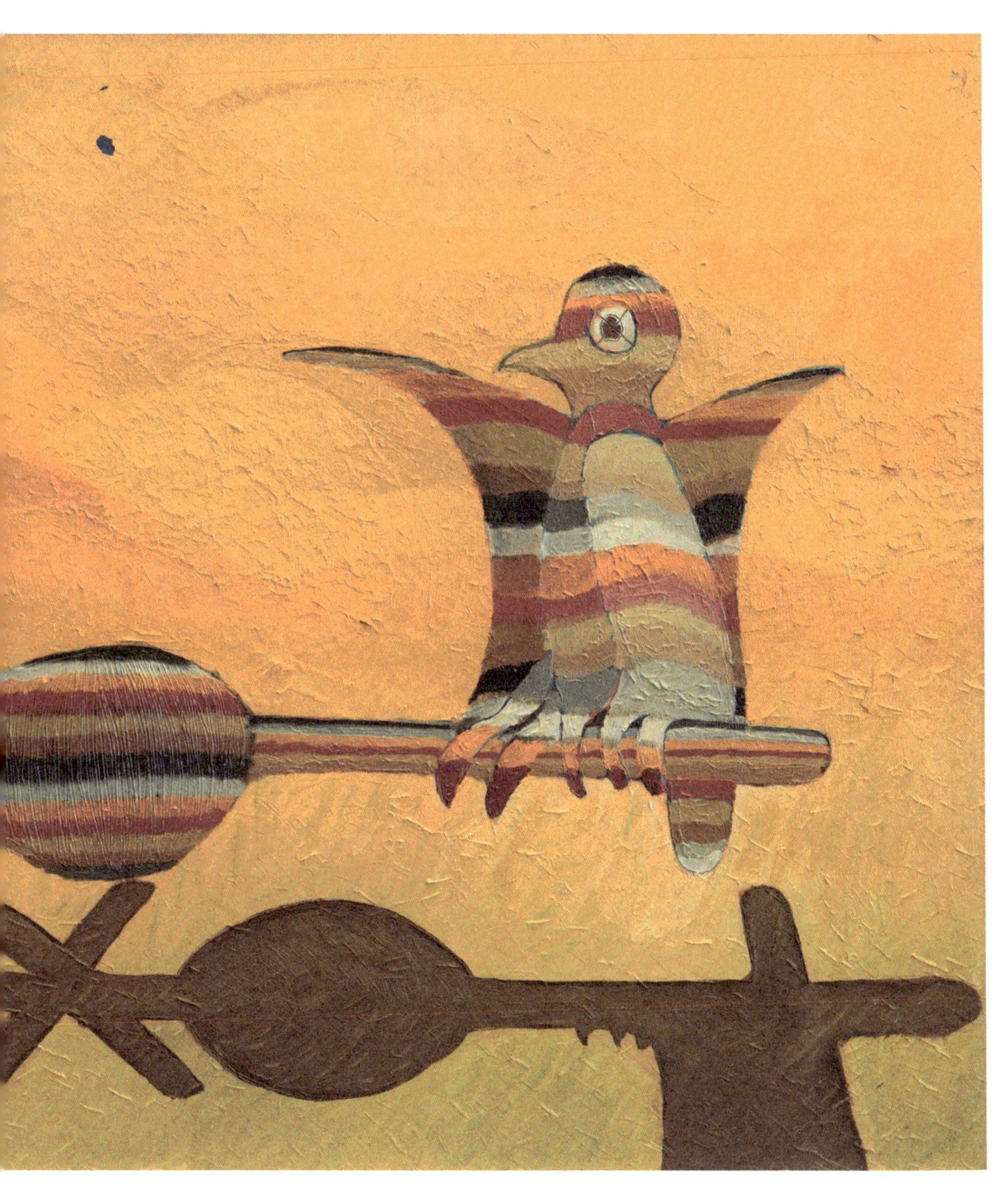

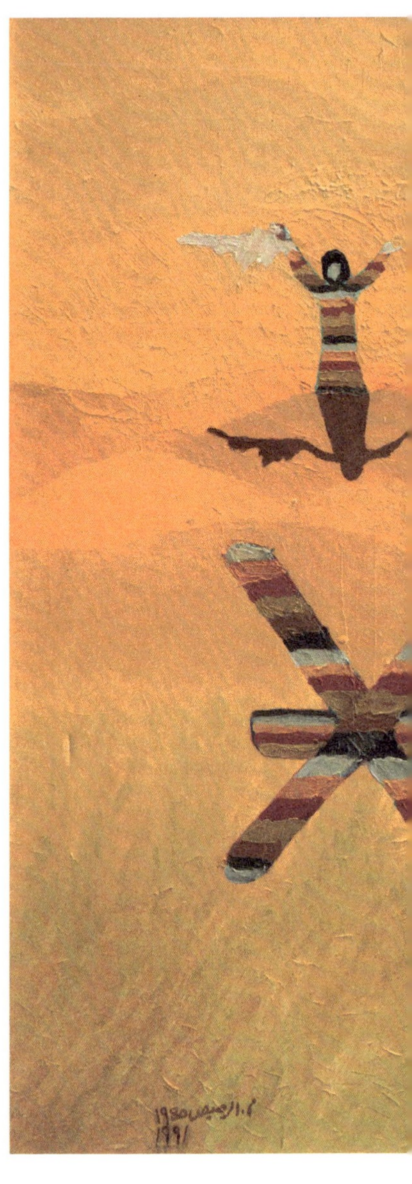

Hawk and Spindle, 1980/1991

Oil on canvas
90 × 120 cm
Courtesy of the artist and Hewar Art Gallery in
Riyadh, Saudi Arabia

الصقر والمغزل، 1991/1980

ألوان زيتية على قماش
90 × 120 سم
بإذن من الفنان وحوار جاليري في الرياض

Bedouin and Spindle, 1981

Oil on canvas
120 × 71 cm
Private collection

بدوية ومغزل، 1981

ألوان زيتية على قماش
120 × 71 سم
مجموعة خاصة

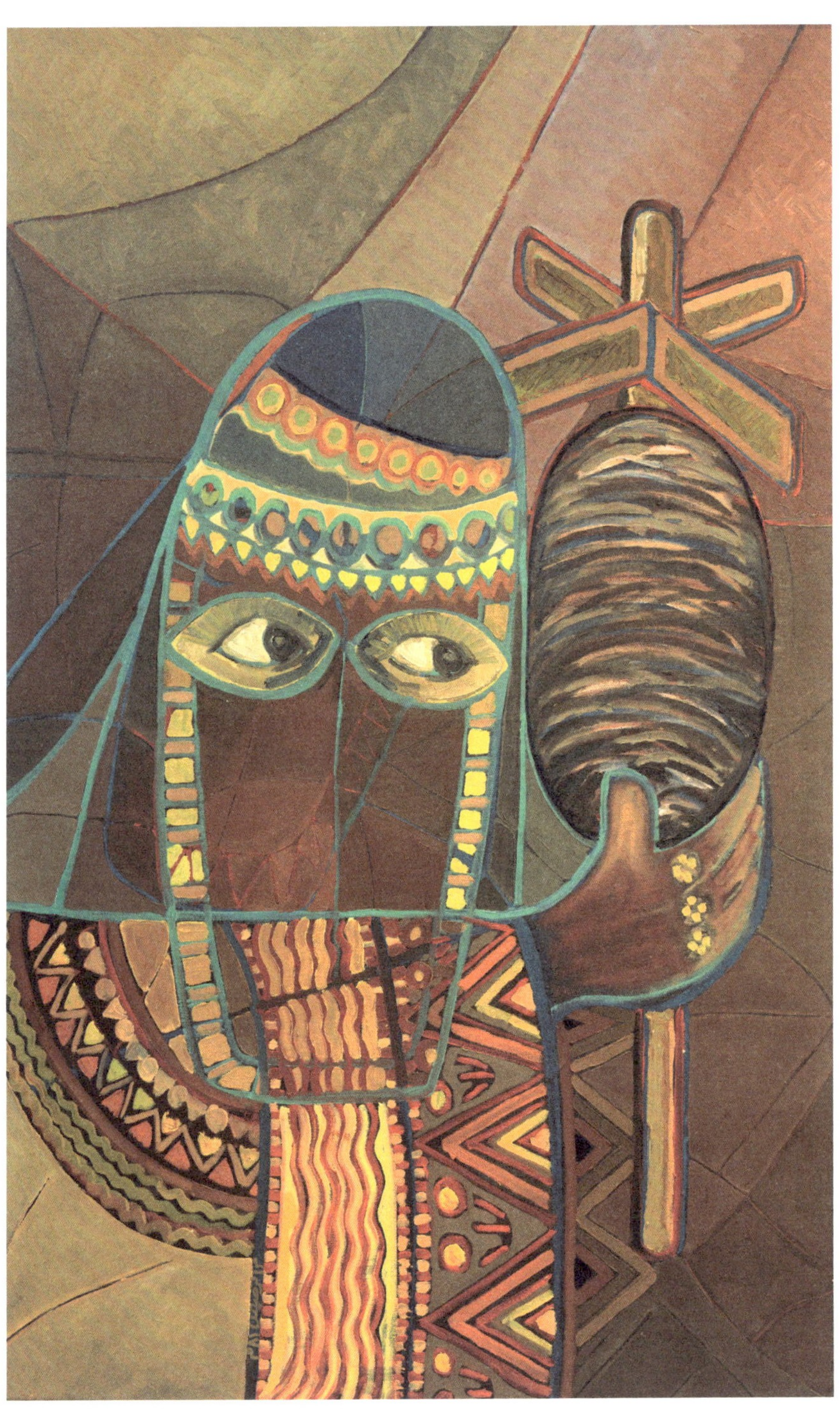

من دراسة «شكل وفراغ»، 1981

خامات متنوعة على ورق
40.5 × 45.5 سم
بإذن من الفنان وصالة تجريد للفنون في الرياض

Form and Space Study, 1981

Mixed media on paper
40.5 × 45.5 cm
Courtesy of the artist and Abstract Art Gallery in
Riyadh, Saudi Arabia

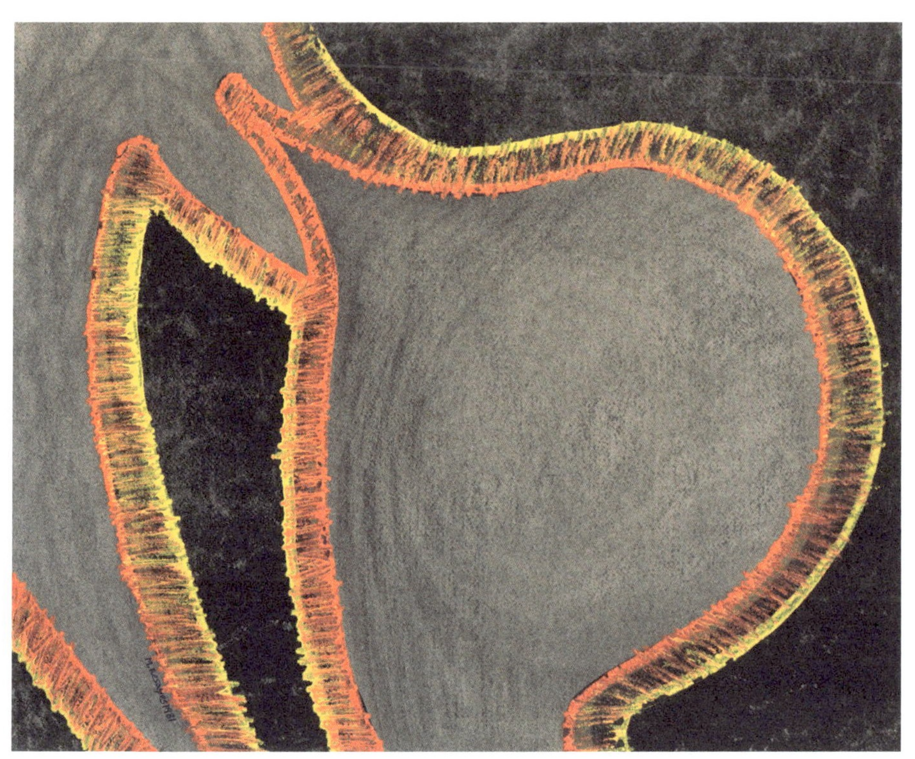

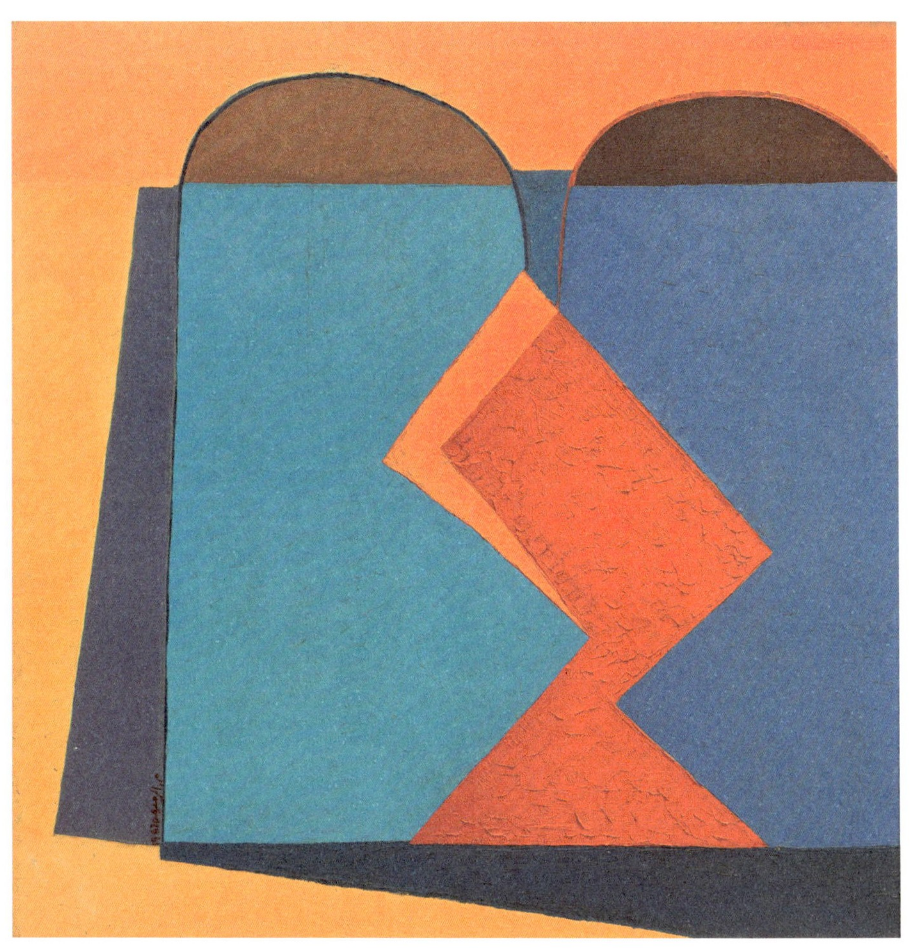

Architectural Elements 4, 1982

Oil on canvas
87.5 × 88 cm
Private collection

عناصر معمارية 4، 1982

ألوان زيتية على قماش
87.5 × 88 سم
مجموعة خاصة

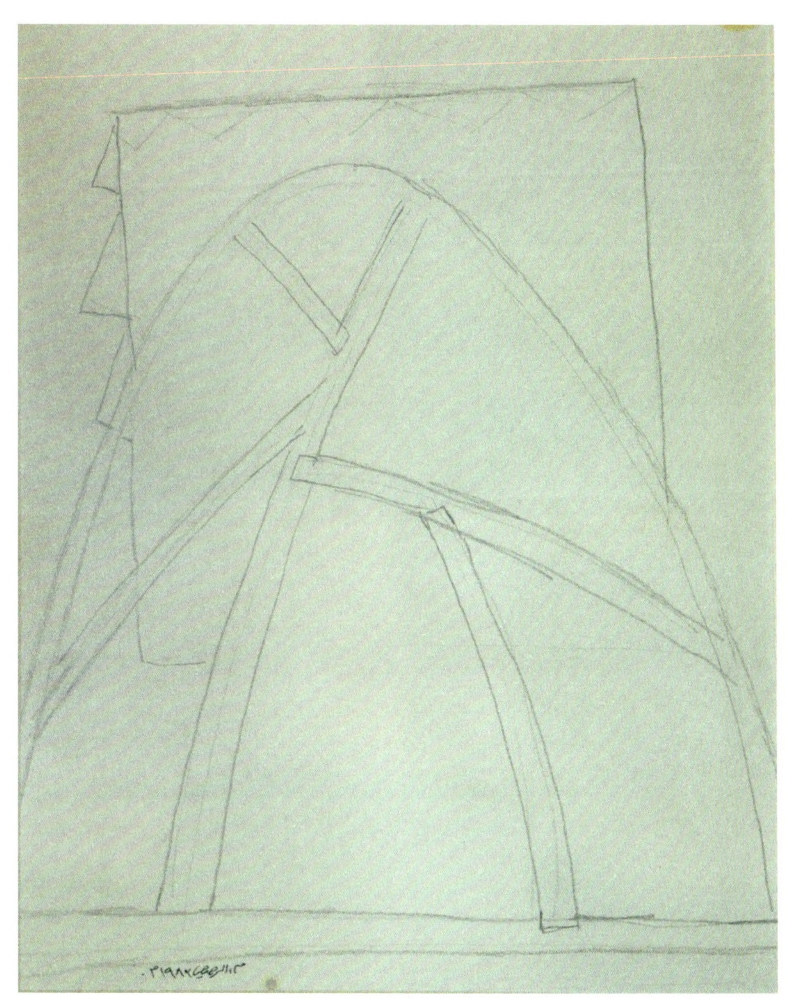

Architectural Elements,
preparatory drawing, 1983

Graphite on paper
37.5 × 29.5 cm
Courtesy of the artist and Errm Art Gallery in
Riyadh, Saudi Arabia

تخطيط أولي
عناصر معمارية، 1983

قلم رصاص على ورق
37.5 × 29.5 سم
بإذن من الفنان وإرم جاليري في الرياض

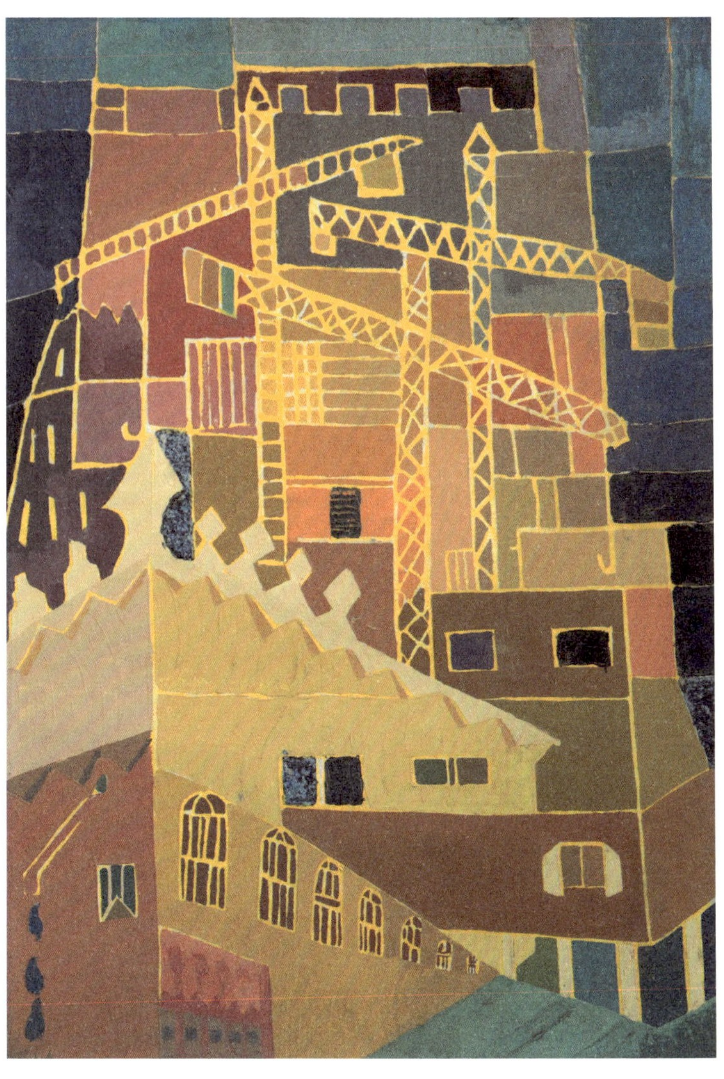

بين القديم والحديث،
1972

ألوان أكريليك على القماش
70 × 50 سم
بإذن من الفنان وصالة تجريد للفنون في الرياض

Between the Old and the New,
1972

Acrylic on canvas
70 × 50 cm
Courtesy of the artist and Abstract Art Gallery in
Riyadh, Saudi Arabia

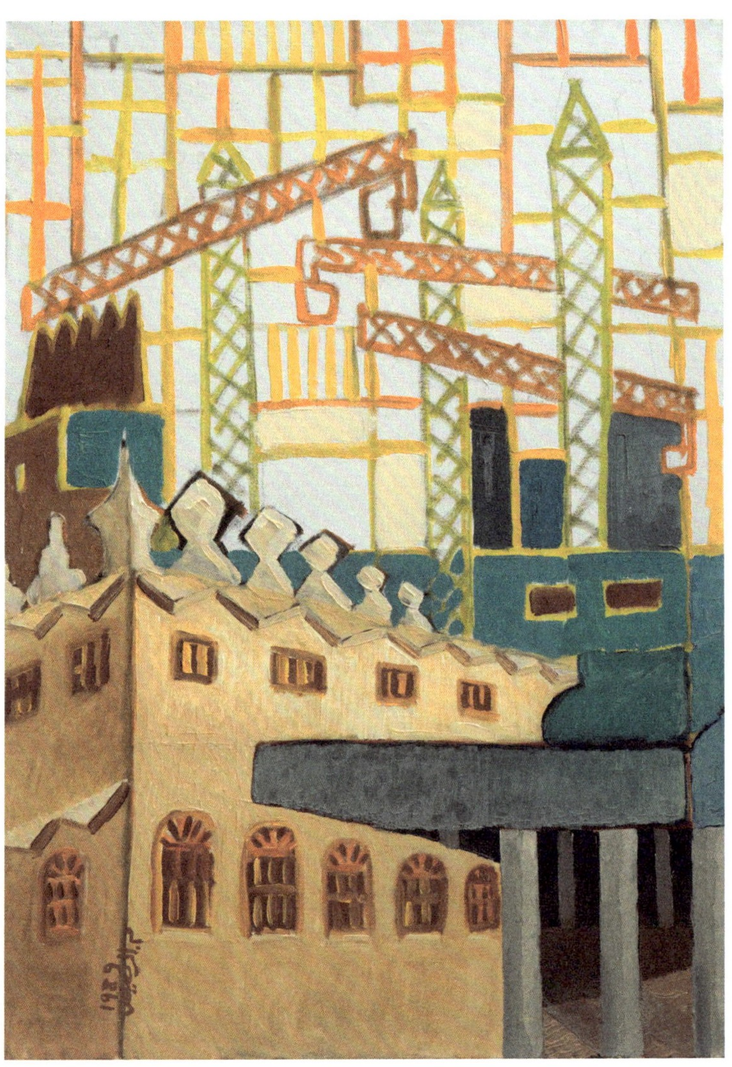

بين القديم والحديث 2،
1989

ألوان زيتية على قماش
70 × 50 سم
بإذن من الفنان وحوار جاليري في الرياض

Between the Old and the New 2,
1989

Oil on canvas
70 × 50 cm
Courtesy of the artist and Hewar Art Gallery in
Riyadh, Saudi Arabia

تكوين معماري 11، 2014

ألوان زيتية على قماش
100 × 150 سم
بإذن من الفنان وحافظ جاليري في جده

Architectural Shapes 11, 2014

Oil on canvas
100 × 150 cm
Courtesy of the artist and Hafez Gallery in Jeddah,
Saudi Arabia

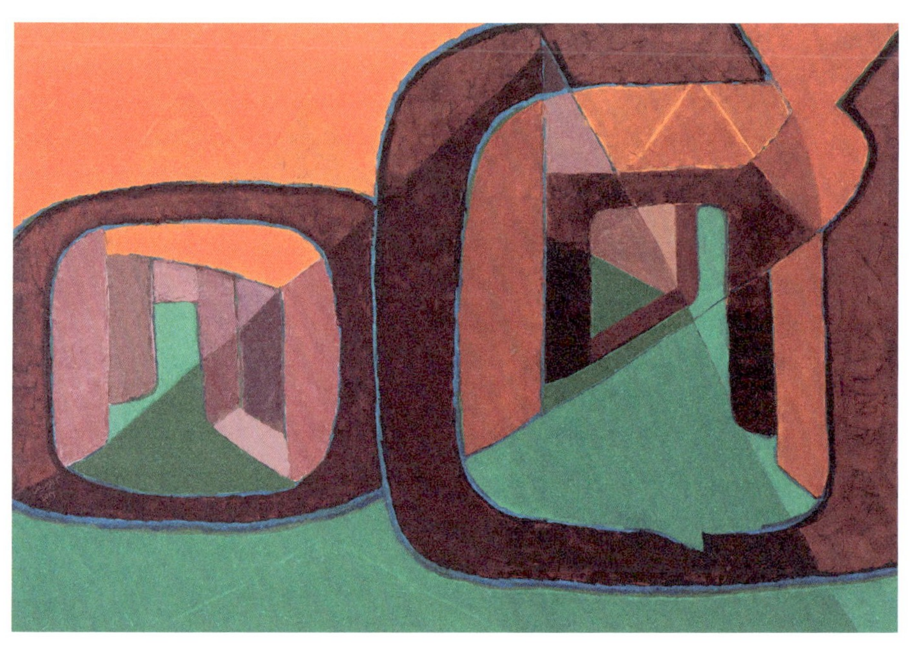

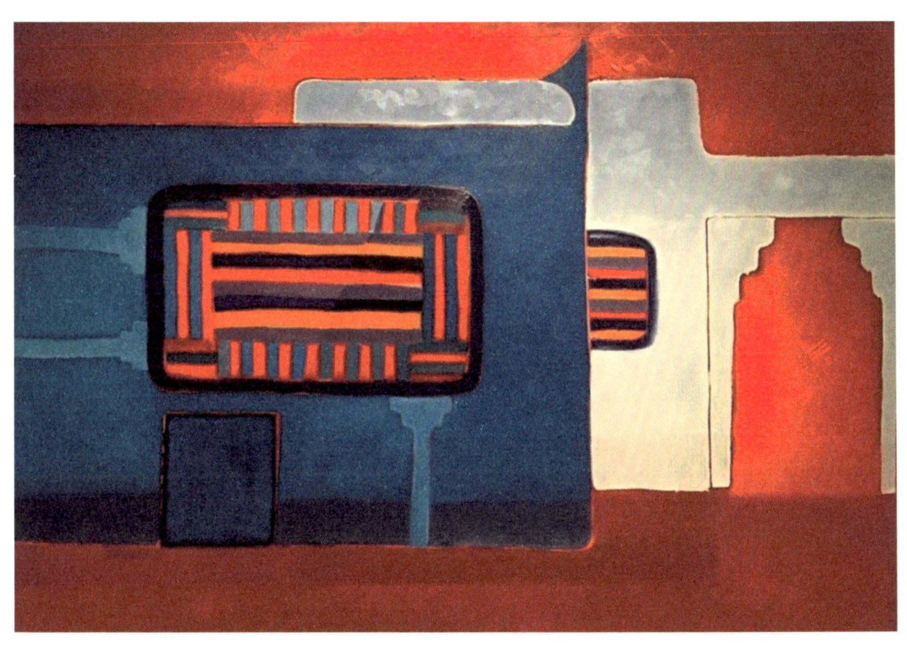

شكل معماري 6، 2014

ألوان زيتية على قماش
100 × 150 سم
بإذن من مؤسسة المنصورية في جدة

Architectural Form 6, 2014

Oil on canvas
100 × 150 cm
Courtesy of Al-Mansouria Foundation in
Jeddah, Saudi Arabia

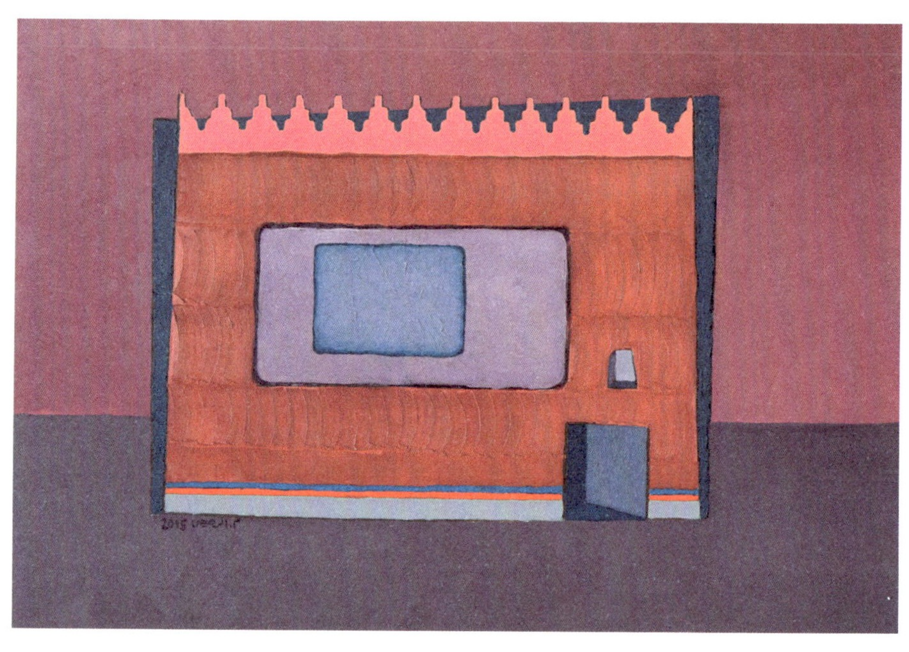

شكل معماري 7، 2015

ألوان زيتية على قماش
150 × 100 سم
بإذن من الفنان وحافظ جاليري في جده

Architectural Form 7, 2015

Oil on canvas
100 × 150 cm
Courtesy of the artist and Hafez Gallery in Jeddah,
Saudi Arabia

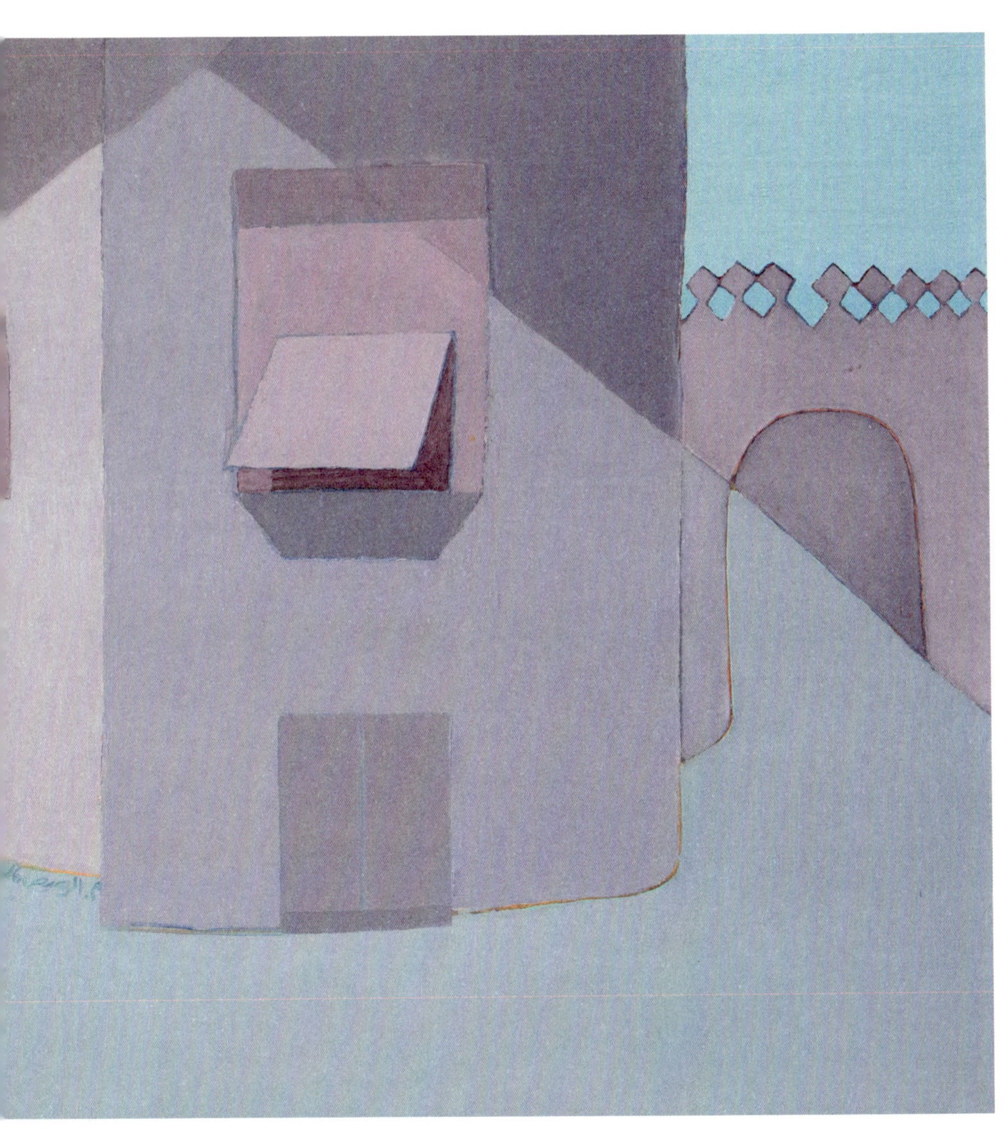

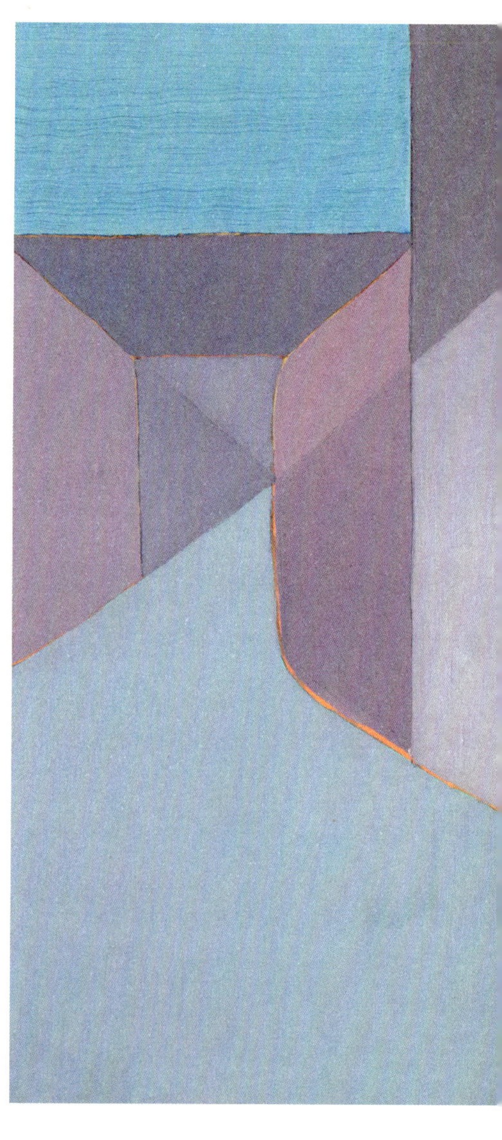

شكل معماري 8، 2015

ألوان زيتية على قماش
150 × 100 سم
بإذن من الفنان وحافظ جاليري في جده

Architectural Form 8, 2015

Oil on canvas
100 × 150 cm
Courtesy of the artist and Hafez Gallery in Jeddah,
Saudi Arabia

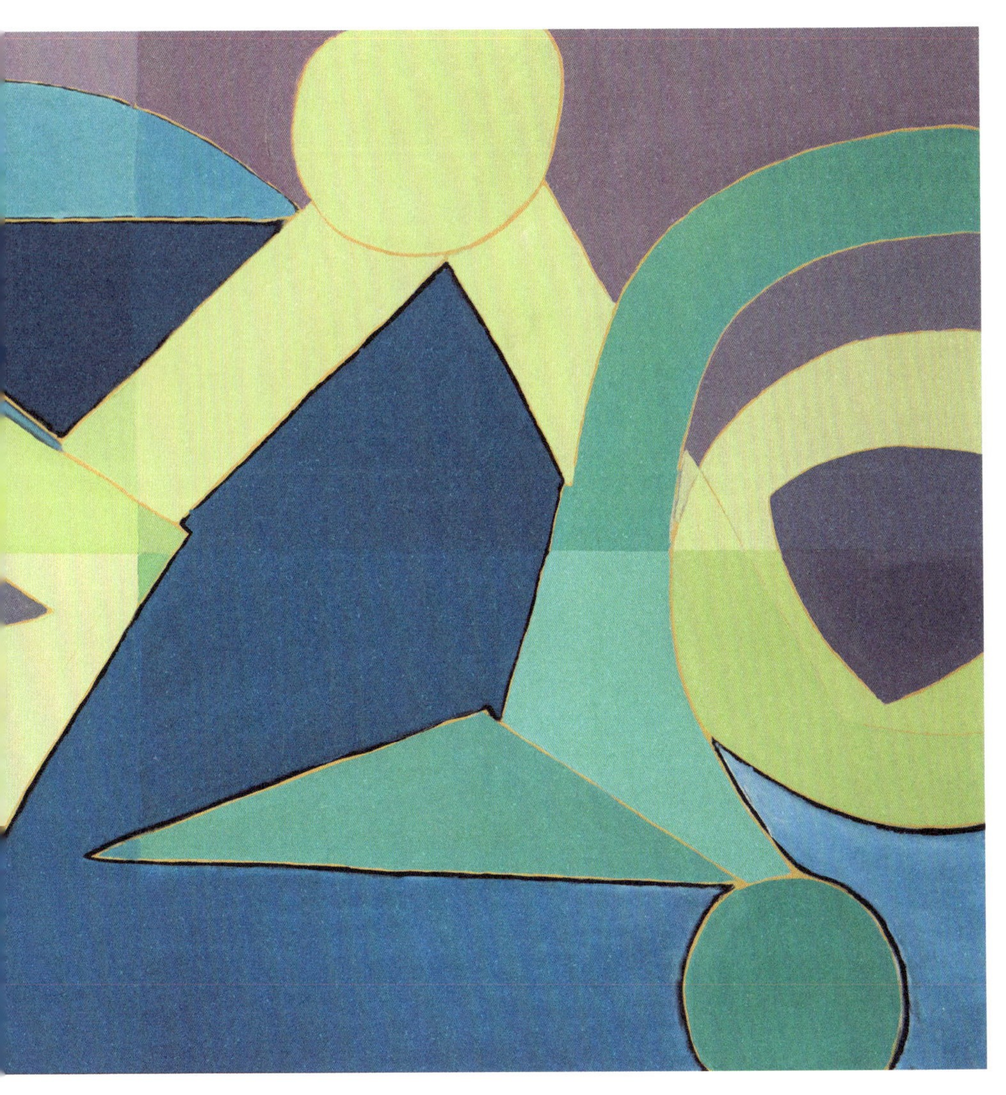

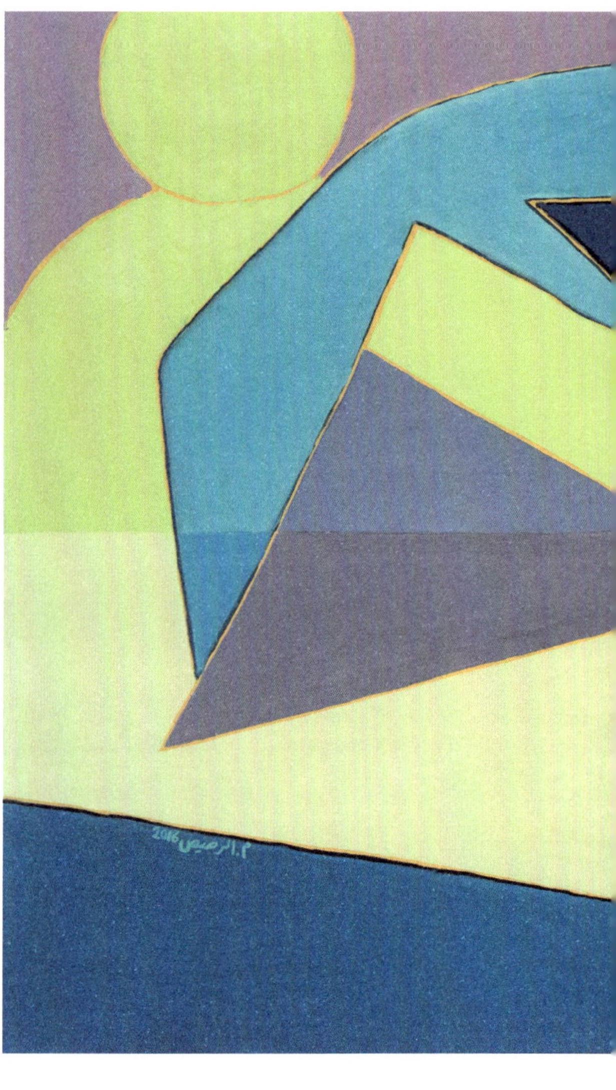

تكوين معماري 12،
2016

ألوان زيتية على قماش
120 × 200 سم
بإذن من الفنان وحافظ جاليري في جده

Architectural Composition 12,
2016

Oil on canvas
120 × 200 cm
Courtesy of the artist and Hafez Gallery in Jeddah,
Saudi Arabia

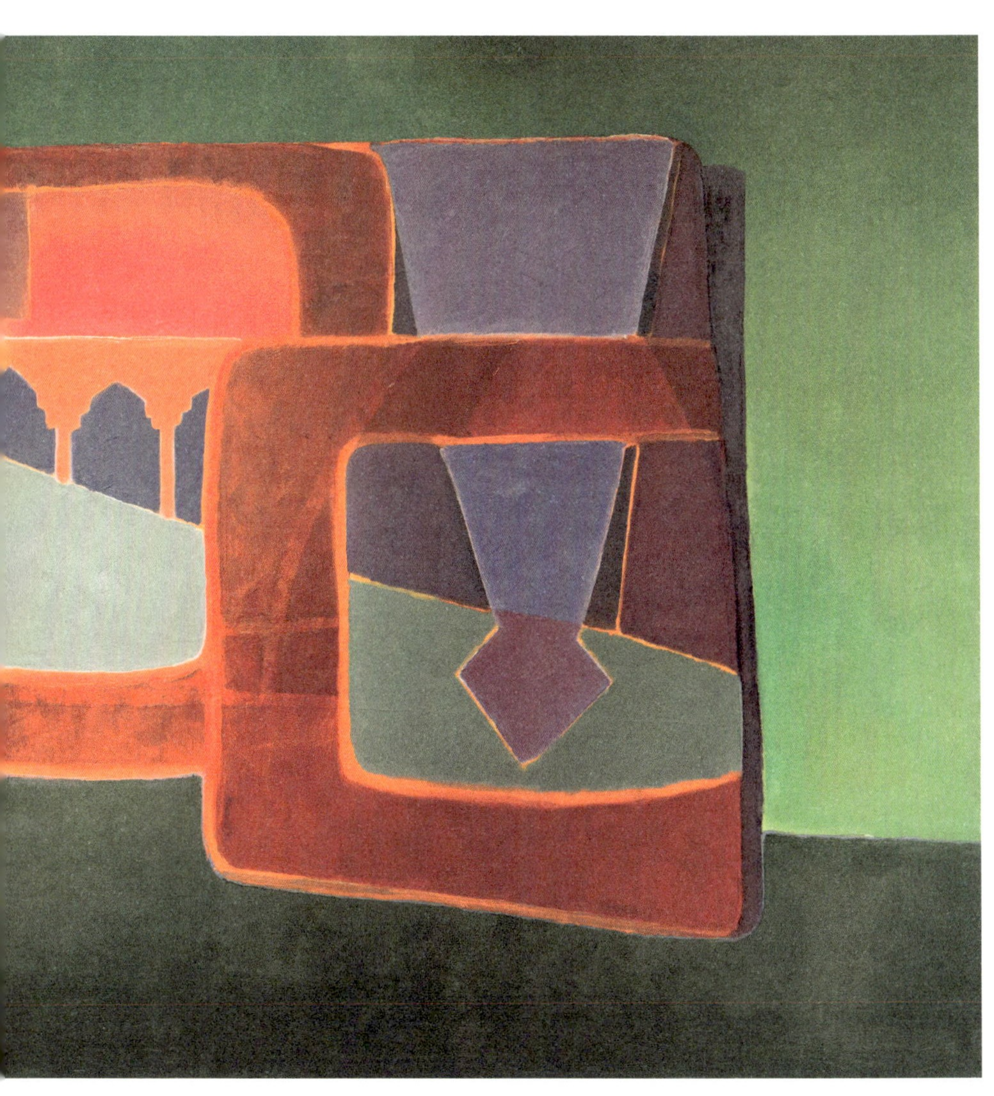

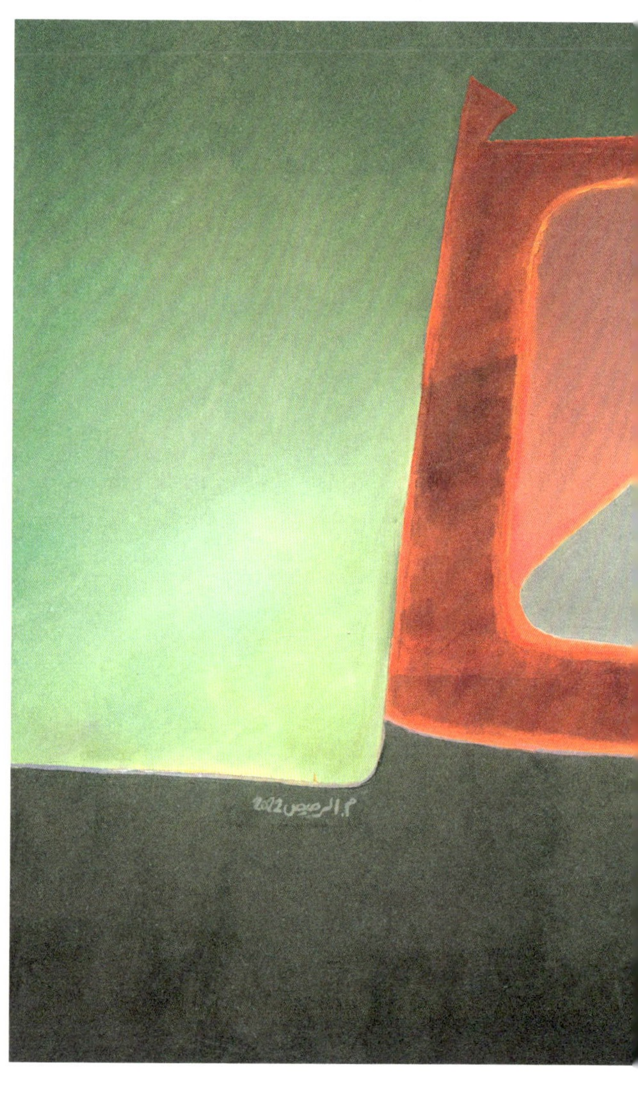

تكوين معماري، 2022

ألوان زيتية على قماش
120 × 200 سم
بإذن من الفنان و015 جاليري في الرياض

Architectural Composition, 2022

Oil on canvas
120 × 200 cm
Courtesy of the artist and 015 Gallery in Riyadh,
Saudi Arabia

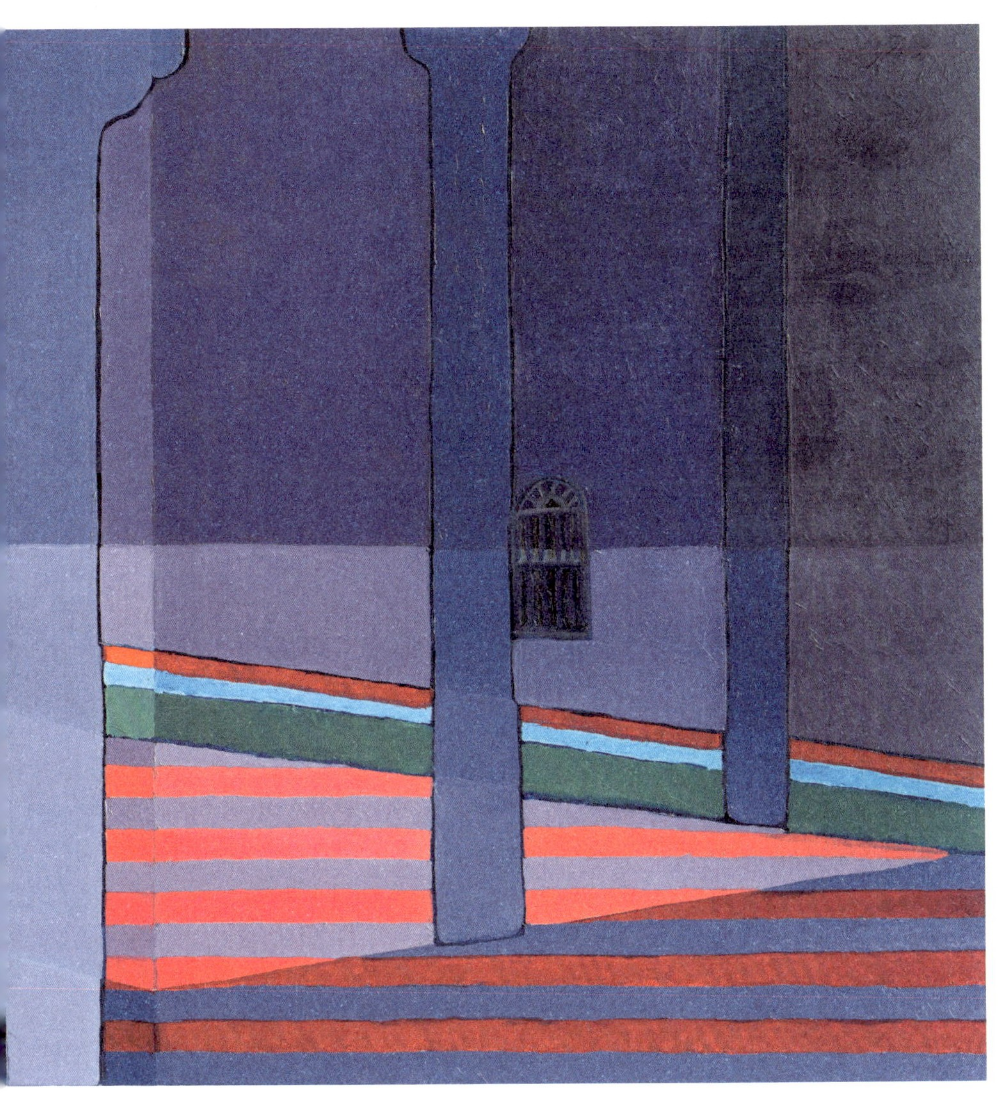

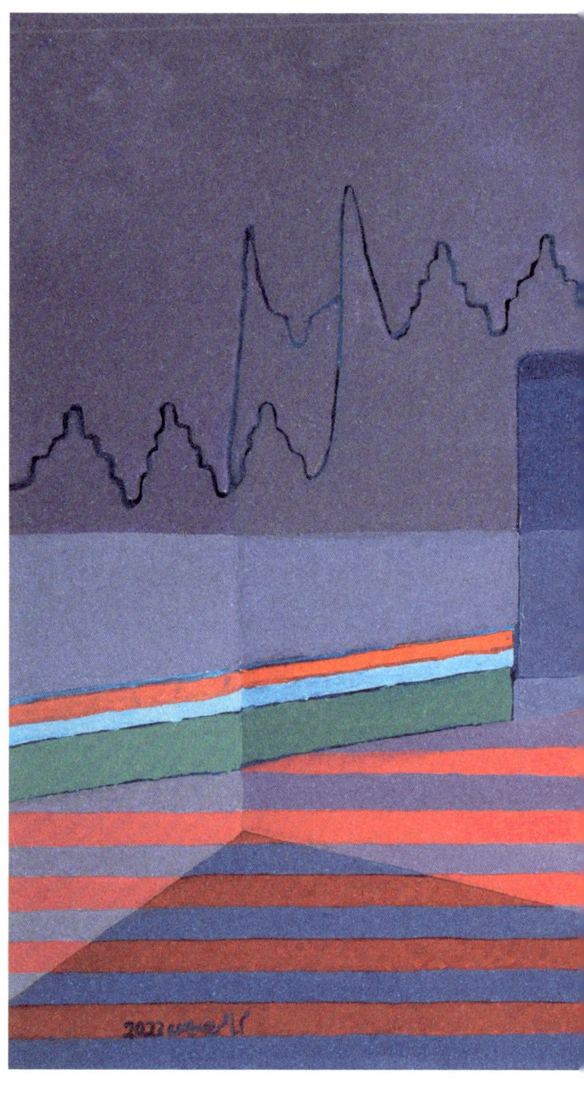

From the *Architectural Elements*
series, 2023

Oil on canvas
100 × 160 cm
Courtesy of the artist and Errm Art Gallery in
Riyadh, Saudi Arabia

من مجموعة
عناصر معمارية، 2023

ألوان زيتية على قماش
100 × 160 سم
بأذن من الفنان وإرم جاليري في الرياض، المملكة العربية السـعودية

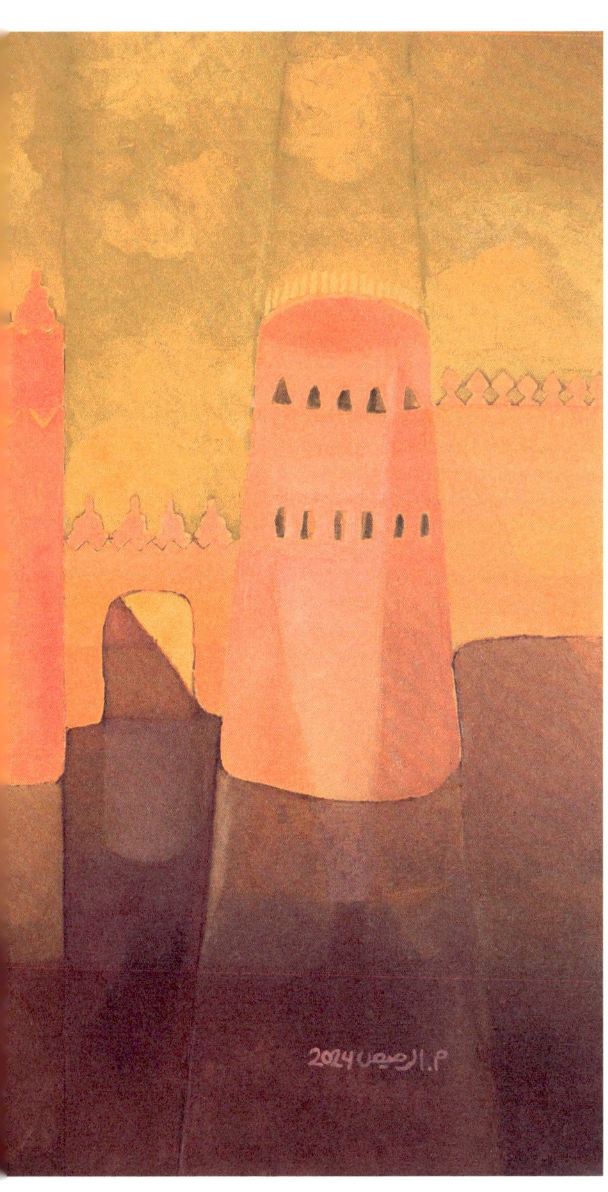

The Return to Architectural Form, 2024

Oil on canvas
100 × 150 cm
Private collection

عودة إلي الشكل المعماري، 2024

ألوان زيتية على قماش
100 × 150 سم
مجموعة خاصة

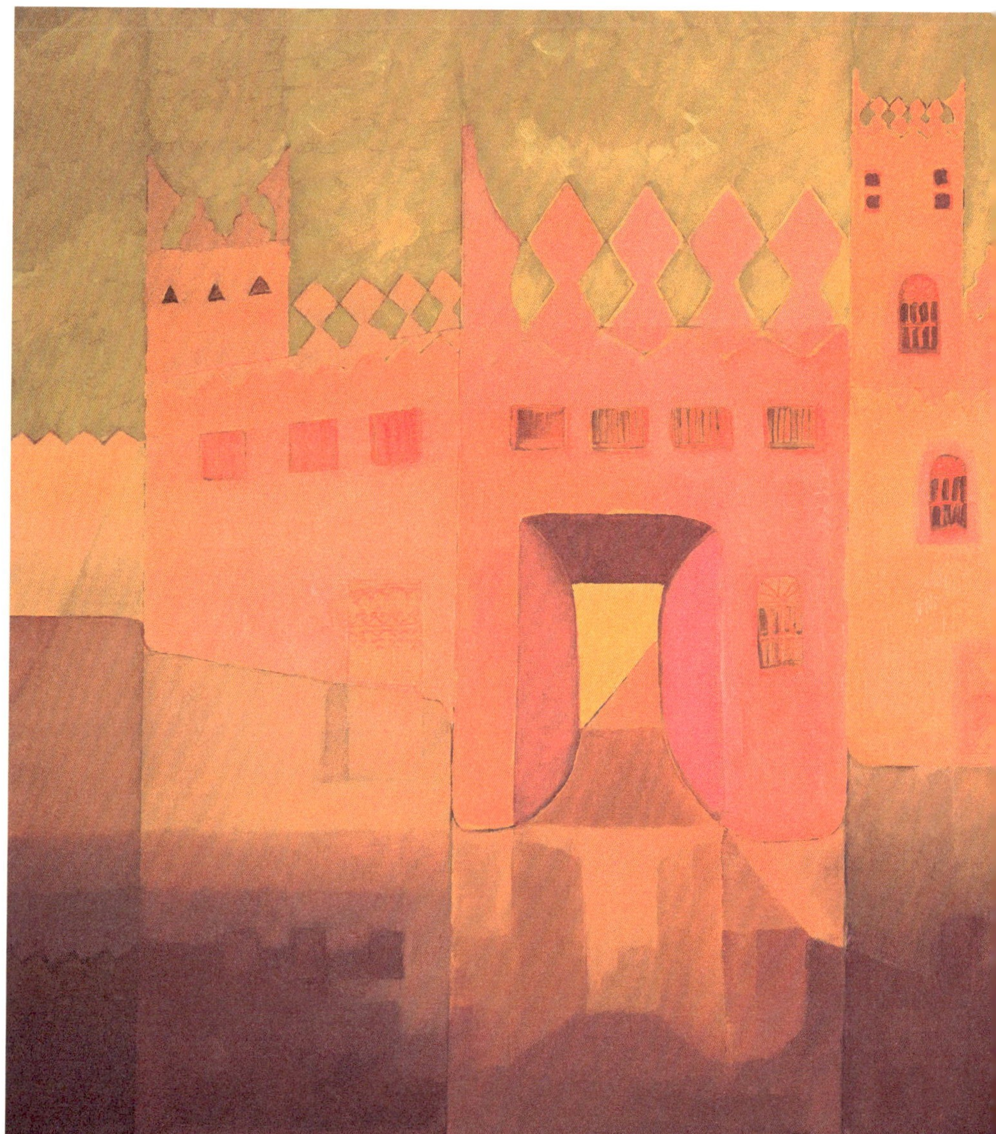

محمد الرصيص: عاشق التراث ومهندس فضاءاته الجمالية الفاتنة

Mohammed Alresayes: Architect of Captivating Aesthetic Spaces

أ.د. معجب الزهراني

Prof. Mojeb Alzahrani

Mohammed Alresayes is of the generation that founded the national visual arts movement in Saudi Arabia. Considering that I have written about him in the past, it would be sensible for me to avoid repetition, in the hope of contributing something novel in relation to his presence in this solo exhibition. I will therefore write from a dual perspective that merges personal, intimate testimony with an objective reading to discuss examples from the rich practice of this icon of the visual arts who has impacted our essentially oral-aural culture. This perspective must be ample and branching, as any retrospective exhibition would present the personal trajectory of an individual artist while recalling the features that their creative practice shares with those of their contemporaries. It would also necessarily offer a glimpse at the broader culture over an extensive period as experienced by the artist, their society, their city, and the world around them. While it is certainly no easy task to engage in deep dialogue with the legacy of a creative individual, a diverse collective artistic memory, and the memory of a rich historical period, it is nevertheless an exciting and rewarding endeavor.

I have known Alresayes to be a serious academic colleague and a serene, kind friend. I have also

محمد الرصيص من جيل أسّس للحركة التشكيلية الوطنية، ونظرًا لكوني قد كتبت عنه من قبل، فمن المنطقي أن أحاول تجنب التكرار عسى أن أضيف جديدًا يخص حضوره في هذا المعرض الاحتفالي، وسأكتب من منظور مزدوج يجمع بين الشهادة الشخصية الحميمة والقراءة الموضوعية المحاورة لنماذج من تجربته الغنية كواحد من رموز هذا الفن البصري المؤثر على ثقافتنا القولية - السمعية في جوهرها. ولابد أن يتسع المنظور ويتعدد بما أن أي معرض استعادي عادة ما يعرض المسار الشخصي للفنان الفرد، ويستحضر معالم التجربة الإبداعية المشتركة بينه وبين زملائه ومن هم في جيله، ويطل بنا ضرورة على الثقافة العامة في حقبة زمنية متسعة عايشها المبدع ومجتمعه ومدينته والعالم من حوله، والمؤكد أنه ليس من السهل الحوار المعمق مع ذاكرة فرد مبدع وذاكرة جماعية فنية متنوعة وذاكرة حقبة تاريخية غنية، لكن المغامرة شيقة ممتعة، وهذا هو الأهم.

عرفت محمد الرصيص زميلًا أكاديميًا رصينًا وصديقًا هادئًا خلوقًا وكتبت عنه مبدعًا مرهفًا خلاقًا ابتكر أسلوبًا يخصه وطور تجربة لا تشبه غيرها. فنظرًا لتقارب منازلنا في سكن جامعة الملك بالدرعية، كثيرًا ما كنا نتلاقى في الحي الجامعي الأنيق أو في ندوات مصاحبة للمعارض التي تنظمها جمعية الثقافة والفنون باعتبارها

described him in writing as a creative, passionate, and innovative individual who has created a unique style and led a distinctive practice. As we once lived in proximity to each other at the King Saud University dormitories in Diriyah, we often met up in the elegant surrounding neighborhood. We also saw each other at seminars that accompanied exhibitions organized by the Saudi Arabian Society for Culture and Arts—an institution he would later head for a short period—which is concerned with the practices of artists of all ages, regions, and aesthetic or intellectual inclinations.

In demonstrating that his artistic practice is distinct, a preliminary question arises: What are the features that distinguish a creative practice from those of other colleagues and pioneers who themselves had an imposing and radiant presence during the same period, including Mohammed Alsaleem, Abduljabbar Alyahya, and Saad Alobaid?

Three factors helped me to produce a preliminary and convincing answer to this question a while ago. Over the course of a decade in the 1980s in Paris, I had successive opportunities to visit the city's museums and write about their activities, including exhibitions for prominent Arab artists, such as Shaker Hassan Alsaid from Iraq, Asaad Arabi from Syria, Rachid Qureshi from Algeria, and Mehdi Qotbi from Morrocco. Upon my return to Saudi Arabia, I built on this experience, participating regularly and multi-facetedly in most of the activities that accompanied exhibitions of this pioneering generation, with whom my relationship gradually solidified, as it did with colleagues and icons of that stage.

Perhaps the most significant material prize of this connection was my acquisition of a collection of paintings, including Mohammed Alresayes's *Traditional Music Band* (1981), Abduljabbar Alyahya's

المؤسسـة الثقافية التـي تعنى بتجارب التشـكيليين من مختلف الأعمار والمناطق والتوجهات الجمالية والفكرية (وقـد ترأسـها فتـرة قصيـرة كمـا نعلم). وحيـن نريد أن نثبـت أن تجربتـه الفنيـة الخاصة لا تشـبه غيرهـا، يظهر التسـاؤل الأولي التالي: ما هي علامات الاختلاف التي تميز تجربة إبداعية شخصية عـن تجارب زملاء ورواد آخريـن كان لهم حضورهم القوي المشـع فـي تلك الفترة كما هـي حال محمد السـليم وعبـد الجبـار اليحيا وسـعد العبيد؟

ثلاثـة عوامـل سـاعدتني علـى بلـورة إجابـة أوليـة مقنعـة منـذ فتـرة طويلـة نسـبيًا. فالحيـاة طوال عقـد من الزمن فـي باريس الثمانينيات التي تعد واحدة مـن المراكـز الكبـرى للفنـون الحديثة، منحتني الفرصـة تلو الأخـرى لأزور متاحفها وأكتب عـن فعالياتها منها معارض لتشـكيليين بارزين من مختلـف البلـدان العربية كالعراقي شـاكر حسـن آل سـعيد والسـوري أسـعد عرابـي والجزائـري رشـيد قريشـي والمغربـي مهـدي قطبـي. وبعـد عودتي، وبنـاءً على هذه التجربة تحديدًا، تنوعت مشـاركاتي المنتظمة في معظم الأنشطة المصاحبة لمعارض جيـل الـرواد حتـى توطـدت علاقاتـي الحميمـة به وبرفـاق المرحلـة ورموزهـا. ولعل الثمـرة الأهـم لذلـك التواصل اقتنائـي مجموعـة مـن اللوحـات التـي أحببتها أكثر مـن غيرها، ومنهـا تحديدًا لوحة «فرقة موسيقية شعبية» (1981م) للرصيص، ولوحة «بناء» لعبد الجبار اليحيا، ولوحة «آية الكرسـي» من آفاقية محمد السليم وأخريات لسعد العبيد ومنيرة الموصلـي. وأعدها الثمـرة الأهم لأن هـذه النماذج الأصليـة أو المصـورة كانت تطل من جـدران منزلي وكثيـرًا ما تغرينـي بتأملها والحوار معها بشـغف لا يُضاهى بالنسبة لأستاذ شاب مولع بالفنون الجميلة ويكتب عنها بأمل أن يترجم مشـاعره ويغـري قـرّاءه وطلابه بمحبة هـذه المنتوجـات الجمالية البصريـة الجديدة علـى المجتمع وثقافتـه آنذاك. هكذا تبلـورت لدي قناعـة عميقة بـأن أهم علامات الاختـلاف التي تميـز أعمـال محمد الرصيـص تنبع من تعلق قديم متجدد بجماليـات التراث العمراني

Building (1983), and Mohammad Alsaleem's inspired work, *Ayat al-Kursi*, among others, and works by Saad Alobaid and Mounirah Mosly. I regarded these acquisitions as the most significant prizes because the works—both originals and replicas—would so often tempt me from their perches on the walls of my home to contemplate and engage them in passionate dialogue. This experience was unrivaled for me as a young professor captivated by fine art, writing about it in the hope of translating my feelings and thus luring my readers and students into loving these aesthetic, visual works, which were then still novel to the society and its culture. I then arrived at a deep conviction that the most prominent features distinguishing Alresayes's works stem from an old and renewing connection to heritage architectural aesthetics in all their visual manifestations, cultural dimensions, and practical as well as spiritual value. He is one of those creatives who is existentially and intimately bound in relation to the spaces of their childhoods. These times in our lives all too quickly alter or vanish, transforming into images, or aesthetic, poetic forms that perennially inhabit the imagination, rouse the senses, and nourish the active fascinations of creativity.

Put differently, most of his works spring from an inner sentimental soliloquy in connection to Riyadh's mud homes, their earthy courtyards and tame creatures, which, whether proximate or distant, shadow him constantly, guiding his thought and spurring his creativity. I will not, of course, delve into the theoretical dimensions of these complex relationships, as elucidated by Gaston Bachelard in his famous philosophical study, *The Poetics of Space*, which has been translated globally and whose ideas have been applied across cultures. I would merely note the prominence of grief as a dimension to such a relationship—and how the work seeks to diagnose it and transform it into a playful aesthetic scene that is pleasing to oneself and to others.

لمختلـف تجلياته البصرية، وأبعاده الثقافية، وقيمه العمليـة، والروحية. إنه واحد من أولئك المبدعين الذيـن تربطهم علاقات وجدانيـة حميمة بفضاءات الطفولة التي سـرعان ما تتغير أو تندثر فتتحول إلى صور وأشـكال جمالية شاعرية تراود المخيلة وتوقظ الحـواس وتغذي هواجـس الإبداع طـوال الحياة.

وبصيغة أخرى نقول إن مجمـل أعماله ناتجة عـن مناجـاة ذهنيـة عاطفيـة متصلة مـع بيـوت الرياض الطينية وسـاحاتها الترابيـة وكائناتها الأليفة التـي ظلـت تخايله وتوجه فكـره وتحفز إبداعاته فـي حالتي القـرب والبعد؛ لـن أخـوض بالطبع في الإطار النظـري لهـذه العلاقـات المتنوعـة المركبة التي بينها «غاسـتون باشـلار» وبلورها فـي أطروحة شـهيرة لم تعد تخفى على أحـد وقد ترجـم كتابه «شـاعرية المـكان» إلـى جـل اللغـات واسـتثمرت أفكاره فـي معظـم الثقافات. نشـير فقـط إلى أن «البعـد المأسـاوي» يحضـر بقـوة في علاقـة كهذه حتمًـا، وأن العمـل إنما يـروم تشـخيصه وقلبه إلى مشـهد جمالي مرح ممتـع للذات وغيرها. فليسـت أزمنـة الطفولة وحدهـا التـي ترحل كحلـم جميل، لأن أطرهـا المكانيـة هي أيضًـا تظل تتغيـر وتتحور وتمحـى، خصوصًـا إذا مـا قدر للـذات أن تعيش في مدينـة محليـة صغيـرة تعرضت لتحـولات جذرية قويـة شـاملة غيـرت معالمها وطمسـت علاماتها لتصبـح مدينة «كوزموبوليتيـة» جديدة خلال عقود قليلة. ثم إن تجربة الرحلات التعليمية المبكرة خارج المكان وبعيدًا عن الأهل مثلت مغامرة استكشافية لا أقل إشـكالية وتعقيدًا ووعودًا، فرحلة كهذه عادة ما تغني الـذات الباحثة المبدعة بمـا لم تكن تعرفه من قبل بقدر ما تربكها وتخلخل وعيها ليتسـع لكل جديد مدهـش مفيد (ولنا أن نتخيـل قوة الصدمة وعمـق الدهشـة والفتى الغـض يشـاهد الأهرامات المصرية أو ناطحات السـحاب الأمريكية لأول مرة). فالبعد المأسـاوي الذي يسمي أشـكال البعد والفقد هو ذاته ما يؤسـس للتجربة الإبداعيـة التي يراد لها أن تعيـن الـذات على مقاومـة الغربـة والتكيف مع الصدمـات الحضارية ومن ثم اسـتثمارها كمجموعة

It is not childhood alone that dissipates like a beautiful dream; its placial outlines also alter, transmute, and are effaced. This is especially true if one were fated to have lived in a small town that undergoes fundamental transformations that in the space of a few decades erase its features to convert it into a new cosmopolitan city.

Moreover, the artist's experience of traveling to study at an early age, away from his place and people, was an exploratory adventure no less tricky, complex, and laden with promises. Such a journey often imbues the creative searcher with what has been thus far unknown to them while also bewildering them and agitating their consciousness to make room for every stunning, instructive novelty. We can only imagine the shock and depth of amazement experienced by a wide-eyed youth peering at the Egyptian pyramids or American skyscrapers for the first time. Grief characterizes some forms of distance and loss, and it is what lays the groundwork for a creative practice through which the self is tasked with resisting alienation and adapting to cultural shocks. The emotion then employs these as a series of forms, colors, and symbols, rearranged in a distinct artwork—all that remains for the self. With the passing of time, these constituent elements, as Jorge Luis Borges posits, gain in significance and vividness. This is precisely what Alresayes experienced and endured, as did an entire generation whose visual, literary, and musical works revolved around a shared collective theme, with each artist having a unique approach marked by the contours of their consciousness and sensibilities. To reveal more of the particularities of Alresayes's oeuvre, one must certainly look closely and explore the details.

On the general technical level, what drew my attention to his work was his stubborn insistence on adopting abstraction in vision, style, and perspective. Moreover, he translates feelings boldly and effectively,

مـن الأشـكال والألـوان والرمـوز التـي يعـاد تشـكيلها فـي عمـل فنـي متميـز هو مـا يتبقـى للـذات وتزداد حضـورًا وإشـعاعًا كلمـا تقدم بهـا الزمن كمـا يقول بورخيـس. هـذا بالضبـط مـا عاشـه وعانـاه محمد الرصيـص وجيـل كامـل تمحـورت أعمالـه البصريـة والأدبيـة والغنائية حول ثيمة عامة مشـتركة قاربها كل مبـدع بطريقـة تخصـه وتعلن محـددات وعيه وذوقـه. ولتبيـن المزيـد مـن الخصائـص لا بـد من تقريـب المنظـور واستكشـاف التفصيلات.

فـي المسـتوى التقنـي العام، لعل أكثـر ما كان يلفـت نظـري فـي أعمـال محمـد الرصيـص ذلك الإصرار العنيد على التجريد الذي تبناه رؤية وأسلوبًا وأفقًـا يترجم مشـاعره ويشـخص تصوراتـه بطريقة فعالة جريئة تعلـن الوفـاء للطفولة وفضاءاتها المفتقـدة لكنها لا تمجد الذاكـرة ولا ترتهن للحنين وإكراهاتـه، فاللوحـة البسـيطة التكويـن المتقشـفة الألـوان فـي الظاهر توحـي فـي العمق بـأن الذات المبدعة ظلت تختبر وتجرب لتبتكر «مقتربًا حداثيا» يمكّنهـا مـن اسـتلهام الأشـكال والألـوان المخزونة فـي الذاكـرة من منظـور جمالي تقنـي محايد يعيد هندسة الأشكال والمساحات بقدر كبير من العفوية والصفـاء والصرامة؛ هكذا يبدو العمل المائل أمامك متصلاً بذاكرة المكان والإنسان بقدر ما هو منفصل مسـتقل بذاته لأنـه لا يحاكي المألوف ولا يسـتعيد المعروف بقـدر ما يختزل ما هو جوهـري فيه. هذا دليـل وعي مبكر بأن الرهان الإبداعي لا يتجسد في فكـرة أو موقف، بل فـي عمل فني متماسـك البنية منسـجم العناصـر، ممتلكًـا لتلـك القـوة الإيحائيـة التي تسـتحوذ على المتلقي وتورطه فـي إغواءاتها، فالعيـن المتبصرة سـتلاحظ في العمـل الواحد كما في مجموعة الأعمال أن العلامات الشـكلية والرموز التعبيريـة الجزئية المتقطعة والخطـوط الهندسـية الممتدة، والمنحنية والمرنة والمسـتقيمة الصارمة؛ تُحقـق التمـازج والتكامل بيـن مجمل العناصر في مشـهد جمالـي -هندسـي يثير الدهشـة والبهجة دون أن يغرقك فـي مضانّ الحنيـن والتفجـع العاطفـي الـذي قـد يتـورط فيـه الفنـان الموجه

embodying visual conceptions in such a way as to declare faithfulness to childhood and its lost spaces without glorifying memory and falling captive to yearning and its shackles. A painting that appears to present a simple composition and austere colors on the surface suggests in its depths that the artist experimented persistently to devise a "modernist approach" with which to summon forms and colors from memory through a neutral, technical, and aesthetic perspective that reconfigures form and space with a great deal of spontaneity, clarity, and boldness. His work thus presents itself as connected to human and placial memory while being equally detached and independently self-contained; it does not speak to the familiar, or recollect the known, but rather, it distills their essence. This attests to an early cognizance that the creative wager is not embodied in an idea or a position, but in an artwork of cohesive structure and coherent constituent elements. These parts are imbued with a power of suggestion that is capable of capturing the audience and ensnaring them in its allure.

The keen eye will note in an individual work or a collection of works that the formal signals, together with the partial, noncontiguous, expressive symbols and the extended, curvy, pliant, straight, and bold geometric lines, achieve a synthesis and complementarity among all the elements, composing an impressive aesthetic-geometric scene. It impresses without smothering one in the glow of yearning and emotional grief that is sometimes the pitfall of an artist guided toward simplistic documentation. To further ascertain the prevalence of this distinctive feature, let us cast a deliberate gaze upon the series of paintings on view in the present exhibition. We will find that, on the whole, they reveal a characteristic that recurs from the early days to the present. At the core is a desire for a creative inventiveness that reconciles the reservoirs of the

بمقاصد التوثيق المبسط، وللتثبت أكثر من هذه الخصيصة المميزة يكفي أن نلقي نظرة متأنية على سلسلة اللوحات المعروضة هنا لنجدها تكشف في مجملها عن سمة تتكرر لديه منذ البدايات حتى اليوم، والسبب أن الناظم العميق هو التوق إلى الابتكار الخلّاق الذي يوائم بين مخزونات ذاكرته وثقافته الأصلية البسيطة المنغلقة ومكتسبات واقع جديد أوسع وأغني هو الذي نمى فيه القدرة على اكتشاف ما يصطخب في العالم من أفكار وتيارات وأساليب تمنح كل مبدع الفرصة كي يتأملها ويحاورها ويستثمرها كما يرى ويريد ويستطيع.

لقد تحولت الصدمات الحضارية المصاحبة لرحلاته التعليمية إلى مصر ثم إلى أمريكا في عقدي السبعينيات والثمانينيات إلى مغامرات جذابة ورهانات مصيرية غيّرت وعي الذات بذاتها الفنية الخلاقة دون أن تشوّهها أو تكسرها، وهكذا انقلبت خيبات الغربة وخساراتها إلى معاناة جدية شاقة للبحث عن طرق تعبير جديدة وتقنيات متطورة تعين الذات على مقاومة الاغتراب والاستلاب أثناء الرحلة، وتعينها على الاحتفال بهويتها الخاصة. وهذه الأعمال ذاتها تؤكد أنها محصلة وعي جديد مرن منفتح يتقن التعبير عن حضوره الفعال بقدر ما يسهم في إثراء الوعي الجمالي وصقل الذوق العام؛ ثم إن استلهام أشكال الفضاءات وألوانها في سلسلة أعمال لا تدعي الاكتمال ولا تنشده، بما أن تسمياتها ذاتها تعلن أنها تخطيطات ومشاريع ومقاربات حرة مفتوحة يراد لها أن تمتع المتلقي بقدر ما تحثه على مزيد من التأمل والبحث والحلم. نعم، قد يولّد التكرار النمطي في عشرين عملاً شيئًا من الملل، لكنه يظل دالًا قويًا على إصرار الذات المبدعة على اكتشاف الجديد الخفي فيما كان عاديًا مألوفًا لمجتمع لم يكن ليستعير المواد والتقنيات من خارج بيئته لمحدودية قدراته ووعيه في الوقت نفسه. وباستثناء لوحتي «الصقر والمغزل»(1980م/1991م) و«تخطيط أولي لشماغ»، (1981م) يبدو جليًا أن الأعمال تترجم ولع الرصيص بإعادة اكتشاف الفضاءات المعمارية

artist's memory and his native, modest, conservative culture with the gains associated with a new, rich, and more expansive reality. These gains have fostered in him the ability to uncover the ideas, currents, and styles permeating the world, there for any creative individual to ponder, interrogate, and employ as they see, wish, or are able.

The culture shocks that accompanied Alresayes on his educational travels to Egypt and the United States in the 1970s and 1980s transformed into compelling adventures and life-altering wagers that stirred within him—without distorting or crushing it—an awareness of an artistic, creative self. In this way, the dismay and loss of estrangement turned into a serious, arduous struggle in search of new forms of expression and advanced techniques capable of aiding the artist in resisting alienation and bereavement along the journey while celebrating his personal identity. The works themselves affirm that they are the product of a new consciousness that is open and supple, adept at expressing its active presence while contributing to the cultivation of public aesthetic awareness and sensibility. Moreover, the conjuring of spatial forms and colors in the collection does not claim or aspire to perfection. The names of the works themselves declare that they are blueprints, projects, or free approximations meant to please the viewer and, in equal measure, urge them to ponder, search, and dream more. Yes, stylistic repetition across twenty works may produce some degree of tedium, but it remains a powerful testament to the insistence of the creative self on uncovering the hidden novelties in what was familiar and mundane. With the exception of *Hawk and Spindle* (1980/1991) and *Shamagh*, preliminary drawing (1981), it is evident that the works relay Alresayes's fervor for

وتشــكيلها، لا باعتبارها فضاءات إنسانية مسكونة أو صالحة للسكنى، بل كأشكال جمالية تثير فيه تلك الدهشــة المحفزة للتجريب والإبداع، بقدر ما توقظ التأمــلات الحرة الممتعــة لدى المشــاهد المتخيل.

إنهــا، وكمــا ألمحنــا آنفًـا، محصلــة مناجــاة عاشــقة متصلة مــع أشكال ومساحات يعاينها المبدع مــرة بعيــن الباحــث المتفكر، ومــرة ببصيرة الفنان المغترب المستكشــف، ومــرات بعين الطفل الشــغوف باللعب بالأشياء ومعها لا غير، ولا مبالغة أو افتعــال هنا، لأن مــن يرى لأول وهلة الفضاءات المعمارية الحديثــة المولعــة بــكل جديد غريــب سيختبر كل المشاعر المتناقضة التي تظل آثارها تعتمل في ذهنه ومخيلتــه لفترة طويلة من الزمن. أمــا أشــكال التفاعــل فمختلفة لدى الــذات المبدعة التي تظل تتســاءل وتبحث وتجرب حتى تســتحوذ على شــيء يخصها من المشــاهد العابرة، فالشــكل العــام عندهـا هــو الأكثـر غرابــة وفتنــة، ومحاولــة اختزاله وإعادة إنتاجه جمالياً هو الرهان الذي يجب كسبه كإنجاز فنيّ يُعرض على آخرين لــم تعد لهم هوية واحدة مبســطة معلقة كما هــي الحال قبيل انطلاق رحلــة التكوين.

ومما يعزز هذه القراءة تلك الأشكال المعمارية القليلة التي تحيل مباشــرة إلى نمــط معماري غربي لــم يكن معروفًـا أو مألوفًـا للعين الجماعيــة إلا بعد عقــود؛ تبــدو لنا هــذه مفارقة مثيــرة للانتباه في سلســلة الأعمال المتجانسة في تســمياتها ودلالاتها العامة مثلها مثــل التخطيطــات التجريدية لوجه الرجل المشــع ألوانًا والمرأة المتشحة بسواد شفيف.

والرصيــص مبــدع طليعــي جــريء يصــر علــى مفاجأة المشاهد المحلي بما يصدمه ويغني ثقافته كذلك المستكشــف الــذي يترحل ويغامــر ويجرب ليفوز بشــيء مختلف يعود به ويعرضه ليمتع غيره ويبرر رحلته ويعوض معاناته، ولا بأس بعد ذلك إن نجح العمل ذاته في تحويل تجربة الذات الفردية المبدعة إلى منجز يفتـح ثقافته الجماعية على أفق جديد قــد يربكها، لكنـه يغنيها ويؤهلها للحوار مع

rediscovering architectural spaces and their compositions, not as human-inhabited or inhabitable
spaces, but as aesthetic forms that kindle within
him an amazement that spurs experimentation and
creativity while inspiring enjoyable free meditation
in the imaginative viewer.

As noted earlier, the work is the product of a passionate soliloquy in connection with forms and spaces
that Alresayes examines. At some times, he does so
with the eye of a musing searcher, at others with the
gaze of an alien artist explorer—and often with the eyes
of a child wholeheartedly toying or playing with things.
There is no exaggeration or contrivance here, as at the
first glance of modern architectural spaces brimming
with all that is new and strange, one experiences the
contradictory emotions whose residues continue to
incubate in their mind and imagination for a long time.
For the creative individual, the forms of interaction
are different, as they continue to question, probe,
and experience until they glean from fleeting scenes
something that belongs to them. The general form is
most strange and captivating to them. Distilling and
reproducing it aesthetically is the wager that must
be won as an artistic accomplishment to be shown
to others who no longer possess a one-dimensional,
suspended identity (as was the case prior to the artist's
journey of composition).

Bolstering this reading is the scarcity in
Alresayes's works of architectural forms directly
pointing to a Western style that would not be known
or familiar to the collective eye at home for decades
to come. This discrepancy is noteworthy in the series
of works bearing consistent names and connotations, such as one depicting the abstract lines of a
man's color-radiating face and a woman shrouded
in translucent black.

العالم الأوسع الذي لـم تره ولم تسـمع بمثله قبلاً،
خاصة وأنهـا تغيرت ولم تظـل هي ذاتها.

أصرّ الصديـق محمـد الرصيص ذات يـوم على
إهدائي لوحة كـرد جميـل علـى مـا كتبته عنـه في
مؤلـف تكريمـي خصـص لتجربتـه، فاختـرت لوحته
«فرقة موسـيقية شـعبية» (1981م) (شـكل 1) التي
ظلـت من أثمـن مقتنياتي، ويسـرني أختم مشـاركتي
بالحوار عن أهم جمالياتها ومصادفة فتنتها؛ فالعناصر
التكوينيـة كلها منفـذة بأسـلوب تكعيبي-وجداني لا
يطمس المعالـم المميّزة لكل عنصر بشـري أو تقني،
بـل يمنحهـا الكثيـر مـن المرونـة الهيكليـة والحيوية
التعبيرية التي تجعل المشـاهد يشـعر بدفء الحفلة
الغنائية الشعبية التي تؤمّنها جماعة محدودة بعيداً
عـن رقابة المجتمـع المحافظ وأخلاقياتـه الصارمة.

عـازف العـود يحتل المركـز من المشـهد وهو
يحتضن آلته بكل جسـده، لا لمجرد شغفه باللحظة
الغنائيـة المخطوفة من زمـن الحياة، بل لأن للعود
ذاتـه دلالات تفيض عـن الوظائف النفعيـة بما أنه
عريـق الجـذور في الزمـن قـوي الحضـور والأثر في
كل تراث موسـيقي عربي.

ويطـل عن يمينه قارع الطبل أو الإيقاع الذي
يمثل هو أيضاً عنصراً شـائعاً في كل مشـهد غنائي،
إلا أنه لا يرقى إلى رتبـة العود بما أنه أقل تطوراً ولا
يتطلب من المهارات فوق مـا يتطلبه من المواهب
وكأنه مجـرد «آلة حرفية» يسـتطيع كثيرون صنعها
واستعمالها والاستمتاع بها.

أمـا عـازف القانـون فهـو الأكثـر تخفيـاً فـي
المشـهد لسـبب مزدوج يتمثـل في غرابة الآلة عن
الاحتفالات الشعبية السائدة، ونادر من يتقن العزف
عليها بكفاءة عالية خارج البيئـات المدنية الحضرية
المتأثرة بثقافات وفنون خارجية وصلتنا ضمن سياق
المثاقفـات الطويلة كمـا هو معـروف، وممـا يعزز
مركزيـة العود وعازفه أن الألوان البنفسـجية والبنية
بمختلـف درجاتهـا علـى أرضيـة المشـهد وخلفيته
كمـا علـى أعضـاء الجسـد العـازف لا تلبـث أن تبرز
حضـور اللـون الأخضـر في جسـد العـود علـى غير

Alresayes is a bold, pioneering artist, and he is insistent on surprising local audiences with things that could jar them and enrich their culture. Akin to an explorer who ventures and voyages, the artist seeks to obtain a novelty to bring home and showcase for the enjoyment of others and to validate his journey as well as offset its tribulations. No harm is done if the same work subsequently succeeds in transforming the journey of the individual creative self into an accomplishment that opens the collective culture up to a new horizon that may bewilder it. In doing so, this "opening up" also enriches the culture and empowers it to engage in dialogue with the wider world, yet unseen and unheard, especially since this culture itself has not remained unchanged.

My friend Alresayes insisted one day on gifting me a painting as an expression of his appreciation for something I had written about him for a publication dedicated to his practice. I chose *Traditional Music Band* (1981) (fig. 1), which remains among my most prized possessions. I am glad to conclude my contribution to this publication with a discussion of the work's aesthetics and my encounter with its allure.

The work's compositional elements are realized in an expressive Cubist style, wherein the artist has not obscured the distinctive features of each human or inanimate figure. Rather, he has imbued them with a great deal of structural suppleness and expressive dynamism, allowing the viewer to feel the warmth of the folkloric song session, secure in an intimate setting away from the conservative community's scrutiny and stringent moral codes.

The oud player occupies the center of the scene, embracing his instrument with his whole body. He is not simply enraptured by a musical moment plucked from the timeline of life, but the oud itself has

توقع، فالأخضر لون الحياة في الشجرة التي صنع منها العود لكنه يبرز هنا كمفارقة تشبه الخرجة في الموشحة الأندلسية التي لا تكتمل وتبلغ ذروتها التعبيرية إلا بفضل اللكنة الأجنبية الغريبة الأليفة بالنسبة لمجتمع طالته الهجنة واستملح حضورها في هذا المقام الفني الماتع.

وغني عن القول إن هيمنة اللون الأزرق الغامق في الخلفية أعلى اللوحة سيذكر المشاهد بأن حفلة هذا الثلاثي الشعبي إنما نظمت في عتمة المساء، إما خشية الرقابة الصارمة، أو لتحفيز التوقعات بما سيأتي به الليل لثلاثي مرح التزم الحذر دون أن يفرط في حقه في المتعة ولسان حاله يردد ما قاله الشاعر محمود درويش «على هذه الأرض ما يستحق الحياة».

connotations that transcend its practical usage: it is deep-rooted in time—a prominent, resonant presence in all of Arabic musical heritage.

To the player's right is a percussionist, a common character in any musical scene. His instrument, however, does not quite reach the stature of the oud, as it is simpler and requires less skill than it does talent—a "craft" instrument of sorts that many have fashioned, played, and enjoyed. For his part, the *qanun* player is the most elusive within the scene, owing to the rarity of his instrument in traditional folkloric settings and the scarcity of proficient players away from urban environments, where outside cultural and artistic influences have made their way over a long history of exchange.

Affirming the centrality of the oud and its player are the hues of purple and brown across the scene's floor, background, and player's body; these colors inevitably and unexpectedly emphasize the presence of green on the oud itself. Green is the color of life on the tree from which the oud is made. But here, it appears as an incongruity, one reminiscent of the *kharija* in the Andalusian *muwashah*, which is incomplete and short of its expressive pinnacle without its vernacular. Foreign and strange, the color is also local and familiar to a society that has embraced fusion and incorporated it into this compelling artistic genre.

Obviously, the dominance of dark blue in the upper background of the painting may remind the viewer that this folkloric trio's session is being held under the darkness of night. It may be so out of fear of stern surveillance or in anticipation of being built throughout the day. As for what the night could have in store for a joyful trio that took precautions without forfeiting their right to enjoyment? To quote the poet Mahmoud Darwish, "On this earth, there is what deserves life."

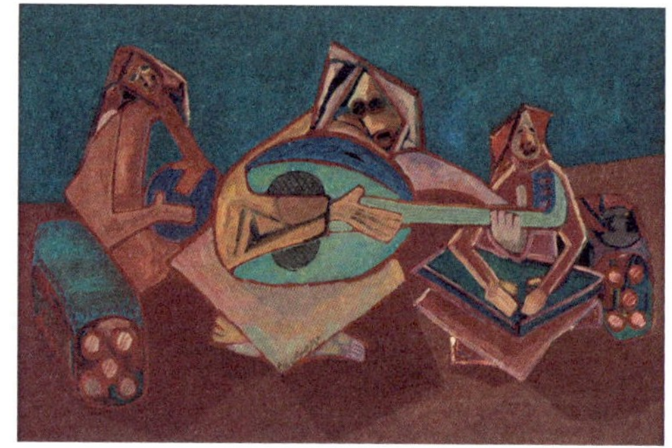

fig. 1

شكل 1

Between Forms

April 23–September 25, 2025
Prince Faisal bin Fahd Arts Hall
Riyadh, Saudi Arabia

Curators
Aram Alajaji, Assistant Curator
at Misk Art Institute
Nada Alaradi, Curator at Misk Art Institute

Art Direction
Amerah Altufail, Art Production Director
at Misk Art Institute

Exhibition Designers
Zahra Zaid, Exhibition Designer at Misk Art Institute
Badr Zabarah, Senior Exhibition Designer
at Misk Art Institute

Translations
Moussa Alhouchi
Omar Odeh

Authors
Aram Alajaji
Nada Alaradi
Prof. Mojeb Alzahrani
Basma Alshathry, Director of Curatorial
Department and Chief Curator

Copyediting
Abdulrahman Sidi, Senior Editor
at Misk Art Institute
Eti Bonn-Muller

Special thanks to the artist, galleries, and collectors for their
invaluable contributions.

بين الطراز

ابريل23- سبتمبر25، 2025
صالة الأمير فيصل بن فهد للفنون
الرياض، المملكة العربية السعودية

القيّم الفني
آرام العجاجي، القيّم الفني المساعد
في معهد مسك للفنون
ندى العرادي، القيّم الفني في معهد مسك للفنون

التوجه الإبداعي
أميرة الطفيل، مدير الإخراج الفني
في معهد مسك للفنون

تصميم المعرض
زهرة زيد، مصمم المعارض في معهد مسك للفنون
بدر زباره، مصمم أول للمعارض
في معهد مسك للفنون

الترجمة
موسى الحوشي
عمر عودة

المؤلفون
آرام العجاجي
ندى العرادي
أ.د. معجب الزهراني
بسمه الشري، مدير عام إدارة التقييم الفني
وكبير القيمين الفنيين

التدقيق اللغوي
عبدالرحمن سيدي، محرر أول
في معهد مسك للفنون
إيتي بون مولر

شكر خاص للفنان والجاليريات والمقتنين على مساهماتهم القيمة

Book Design and Layout
-scope Ateliers

English Proofreading
Zeina Assaf

First edition, 2025
© Kaph Books, 2025
© Misk Art Institute, 2025

ISBN: 978-614-8035-77-7

Printed in April 2025

Published by

www.kaphbooks.com

Distribution
NORTH AMERICA - LATIN AMERICA - ASIA - AUSTRALIA
ARTBOOK | D.A.P.
75 Broad Street, Suite 630
New York, NY 10004
www.artbook.com

FRANCE - SWITZERLAND - BELGIUM - LUXEMBOURG
Les Presses du Réel
35 rue Colson,
21000 Dijon, France
www.lespressesdureel.com

REST OF EUROPE
Idea Books
Nieuwe Herengracht 11
1011 RK Amsterdam, The Netherlands
www.ideabooks.nl

MIDDLE EAST
CIEL BOOK DISTRIBUTION
Al Manara Road, Al Quoz 1, P.O. Box 282005
Dubai, United Arab Emirates
www.ciel.me

تصميم الكتاب وتنسيقه
-سكوب أتلييه

المراجعة اللغوية العربية
محمد حمدان

الطبعة الأولى، 2025
© كتب كاف، 2025
© معهد مسك للفنون، 2025

ردمك: 978-614-8035-77-7

طُبع في نيسان 2025

النشر من قبل

www.kaphbooks.com

التوزيع
أمريكا الشـمالية - أمريكا اللاتينية - آسيا - أستراليا
ARTBOOK | D.A.P.
75 شارع برود، جناح 630
نيويورك، نيويورك 10004
www.artbook.com

فرنسا - سويسرا - بلجيكا - لوكسمبورغ
Les Presses du Réel
35 شارع كولسون،
21000 ديجون، فرنسا
www.lespressesdureel.com

بقية أوروبا
Idea Books
نيووي هيرنغراخت 11
RK 1011 أمستردام، هولندا
www.ideabooks.nl

الشرق الأوسط
CIEL BOOK DISTRIBUTION
شارع المنارة، القوز 1، ص.ب 282005
دبي، الإمارات العربية المتحدة
www.ciel.me